DREAMS <u>DO</u> COME TRUE!

Call them mini-miracles, call them revelations, but relax, enjoy and listen as Betsy Patterson tells the very special story of a most unusual faith. This is more than autobiography—it is a guide to the healing power of Christ and proof positive that **the lost can be found!**

Singles, parents and families alike will be enriched by sharing Betsy Patterson's understanding of God's Top Drawer Secrets—the power of confession, the quiet time, the faith within; strength in the face of tragedy; the discovery of joy in sadness, and the true appreciation of life that comes from total commitment.

<u>"The spirit-filled Christian is contagious. . . . I have had my trials during these past twenty years, but never once did God make me walk alone."</u>

THE VALLEY
OF VISION

Betsy Patterson

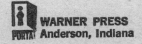 **WARNER PRESS**
Anderson, Indiana

To the honor and glory of God the Father
God the Son
God the Holy Spirit.

THE VALLEY OF VISION

A PORTAL BOOK
Published for Warner Press, Inc., by Pyramid Publications

Portal Books edition published September, 1973
Second printing December, 1973

ISBN 0-87162-161-4

Printed in the United States of America

PORTAL BOOKS are published by Warner Press, Inc.
1200 East 5th Street, Anderson, Indiana 46011, U.S.A.

CONTENTS

ACKNOWLEDGMENTS

My words cannot express the joy and thankfulness that has been mine for the help of my neighbor and dear friend, Mil Gerig, who has spent hours at her typewriter typing this manuscript, and for Carol Seaman, a wonderful friend, who has spent hours with me editing it. For this efficient and loving help and for all the prayers, encouragement, and love from all of my friends, God's words best describe what's in my heart, "Ointment and perfume rejoice the heart, so doth the sweetness of a man's friend" (Proverbs 27:9).

FOREWORD

It's interesting how God puts people together in his beautiful plan for our lives. And I'll never forget the day Betsy walked into my life, or I suppose I should say I walked into her life because she was sitting down! I don't know what drew me to Betsy except the hand of God himself. Several of us had lunch together that day—a luncheon date none of us will ever forget because of the Presence of God which was so real.

I particularly remember Betsy because of her shining countenance and the love of God which just flowed from her face. Here was a woman, I later discovered, who had been through the deep waters and had come out victorious!

This book will bless your heart as she shares from her innermost being the joys, the sorrows, the happiness, the agony of one who is totally committed to Christ. Through the entire book you will see the thread of her beautiful faith and trust in God, never wavering, but strengthening each time, each day, each moment as life brings what it does.

To any mother who has ever shared the tragedy that Betsy went through, this book will give you courage and warm your heart through and through as you see what the abiding love of Jesus Christ can do in circumstances like this. You'll also notice how her faith has grown in a beautiful way over the years. This deep commitment was not because of a tragedy, but rather in spite of it. It seems as though her faith would have grown with or without tragedy which is the way we must be before God. Loving him, serving him, sharing him, accepting his plan for her life without question, Betsy displays that beautiful gift of faith at all times.

Whether you're facing a problem, or whether you're coasting with Jesus right now, read this book! It will lift you up, because it lifts him up!

Because of him,

Frances E. Hunter

INTRODUCTION

I have a "real thing" about introductions to books. I love them! I never read a book without first read-why the book was born. Since you probably feel the same way, let me share with you how this book came into being.

After I became a Christian the Lord impressed upon me that he wanted me to write a book. I thought I would begin writing immediately but never dreamed the "go" signal would be delayed for fifteen years. Throughout these past years I have learned that God's timing is not our timing. As I related experiences I had with the Lord, several of my friends urged me to write a book, but I knew if I were to obey him I must wait until I had definite guidance. In seeking definite guidance I've learned there should be harmony in three different areas. These areas are God's Word, circumstances, and one's own feelings.

I was convinced God wanted me to write a book because from time to time he continued to give me verses telling me just that. I still needed circumstances and my own feelings to complete the picture. The first verse he gave me was Jeremiah 30:2, "Write thee all the words that I have spoken unto thee in a book." Another time he gave me Isaiah 8:1, "Take thee a great roll, and write in it with a man's pen." While spending some time in California, I received a letter from a friend in which she enclosed a verse, stating it was just for me. It was Job 19:23, "Oh that my words were now written. Oh that they were printed in a book." It was then I made the decision to keep notes on the different experiences the Lord was giving me and the truths I was learning through these experiences. Another verse he gave me was Habakkuk 2:2, "Write the vision, and make it plain upon tables, that he may run that readeth it."

As I was waiting on the Lord, I prayed that he might send someone into my life who would bring about the circumstances and the "go ahead" feelings I yet needed. Two years ago while on a fun trip to San Antonio, Texas I happened to go into a Christian book store located across the street from our hotel. As I was browsing through this store, my eyes fell on a book entitled *God Is Fabulous*, by Frances Gardner (now Hunter). Since I, too, believe God is fabulous I knew I *had* to read this book. I bought it, took it back to the hotel, read it, laid it down, and said, "Lord, this is the kind of book, with your help, I could write." Two years later God initiated a set of circumstances that brought Frances Gardner into my life to become my encourager and dear friend. Only God could have engineered these circumstances.

It all began like this. Another Frances asked me if I would take a speaking engagement that she was not able to accept because of a prior commitment. Being free that night, I accepted. When I had finished speaking, it was announced that Frances Gardner, author of the book *God Is Fabulous*, was going to be in the area for a speaking engagement. I pricked up my ears. Since I had read her book and had given numerous copies to my friends, I wanted to meet this *one* Frances Gardner. However, that particular week I was so busy I just didn't see how I could attend. In fact, I really had given it up, but God had other plans.

During my "quiet time" on Wednesday morning before Mrs. Gardner was to speak on Friday, the Lord impressed me with the thought that he wanted me to go and hear Mrs. Gardner and the reason was "the book." I had told several of my friends about this meeting. On Thursday one of them called me and said, "Let's go to hear Mrs. Gardner." I answered, "Let's do." She said a mutual friend of ours also wanted to go.

While we three were on our way I had a little conversation with the Lord, but I will say it was one-sided. I was doing all the talking. It went something like this:

"Lord, I really can't see how my going to hear Mrs. Gardner is going to help me with "the book". She speaks to hundreds of women and I will be just another woman to her. If I mention that I believe you want me to write a book I just know she'll think, 'Oh, yes, here's another woman who wants to write a book.' Lord, you know I will feel so foolish when she turns me off. I really hesitate to bother her with this and, too, when would I have an opportunity to say anything to her? So many women will want to speak with her." I finally said, "Lord, it's in your hands."

To my utter amazement the format of the meeting was completely different from any meeting of this kind I had ever attended. After everyone was seated Mrs. Gardner came in from the back of the room and even though that room was filled with women, she went to each woman and greeted her personally. I was next in line. My heart began to pound. The Holy Spirit whispered into my ear, "Now is your opportunity. Tell her about the book." I did. She was exuberant in her response and said she would love to talk to me about writing. As she was speaking I thought, 'Wouldn't it be great to have lunch with her?' Immediately I dismissed that idea feeling it might be selfish on my part.

After the closing prayer, one of my friends leaned over to me and said, "Why don't we ask Mrs. Gardner to have lunch with us?" I felt this was a confirmation of my own thoughts. As we were leaving we asked her if she would come and have lunch with us. She responded with enthusiasm in the affirmative but said she had a radio interview at noon; however, she would be free after that. The three of us tagged along to the radio station. Suddenly I remembered I was to be at my husband's office at two o'clock. (He is a doctor and I am his office nurse.) Oh, how I hated to mention this to my friends. I knew they would be reluctant to leave the luncheon at the height of the conversation. I decided to call the office to see how many patients were coming in. When the reply was, "No patients are coming in this afternoon," I realized once again the Lord had intervened. I thanked and praised him for these circumstances.

The radio interview was over and we were to proceed to the restaurant in two separate automobiles. I got into the back seat of my friend's car. The next thing I knew Mrs. Gardner was sitting with me in the back seat. On the way to the restaurant I asked her, "How do I begin to write a book?" She said simply, "Sit down at your typewriter and hang loose with Jesus." After receiving her enthusiastic response to my questions and comments, I suddenly felt very excited and very anxious to begin. That phrase "hang loose with Jesus" kept repeating itself in my mind. The luncheon was over and we were saying our goodbyes. Frances put her arm about me and said, "I'll be back in January for another speaking engagement and I will want to read the first chapter of your book." I returned home excited, thrilled, and very happy. I truly believe God had permitted Mrs. Gardner to come into my life to provide the circumstances and the personal feelings that are so necessary for definite guidance.

The next morning the Lord again gave me confirmation in his Word. I was led in my Bible reading to Isaiah 30:8, "Now go, write it before them in a table, and note it in a book, that it may be for the time to come for ever and ever."

It was in the busy days of December when I shared this whole story with my husband. He said, "Honey, you surely aren't going to start on that book now." I didn't know exactly the time I would begin but I was sure the Lord would tell me. I knew that regardless of when it was, I would obey.

How did the Lord let me know? Again I agree with Frances, who is now Mrs. Charles Hunter, that God is fabulous. On Saturday morning, January 3, in the quietness of my husband's office while I was praying and reading his Word, these words in Psalm 39:7 fairly leaped from the page:

"And now, Lord, what wait I for? my hope is in thee." Praise the Lord! The time was right. I had the go signal. Yes, I did begin this introduction that very day. I can only say, "Thank you, Lord, for giving me the grace and patience to wait fifteen years upon thee."

Isaiah 40:31 "But they that wait upon the Lord shall renew their strength; they shall mount up with wings as eagles; they shall run, and not be weary; and they shall walk, and not faint." I believe every word of this promise. Now, "the book."

CHAPTER I

WHENCE I CAME

Sometimes we have to be taken down into the "Valley of Vision" before our eyes can be opened to the truth, the real truth, nothing but the truth.

"And ye shall know the truth, and the truth shall make you free."
—John 8:32

"Help me, God, oh, please help me!" One Saturday afternoon about nineteen years ago, God looked down from his heavenly throne and saw a little speck of humanity on her knees. I was at the end of myself and I was calling out to God. God looks upon the heart, and he knew that I was sincere, that I wanted and needed *his* help. I got up from my knees believing he was going to help, but I didn't know how. That very moment God set into motion a chain of events that led me into a personal encounter with Jesus Christ. I had to look full into his face and make a decision. Little did I realize then the *importance* of that decision and the change it would bring about in my life. It is about this change and what God has done in me and through me that I would like to share with you.

The beginning of my life is not unlike others who have a story to tell about our miraculous God. I was reared in a Christian home. In fact, I believe I was in church more than I was out of it. Mother would always take me to the Wednesday morning prayer meeting with her. We would drag my little red chair along and I would sit at her side. I had a wonderful childhood and grew up with a loving and concerned mother and dad. In retrospect, I am convinced I received some special attention since I was the only girl in a family of four boys. I always felt very close to both my mother and my dad. There certainly was no communication gap in our relationship. To mother I will be eternally grateful for the time she took to read to me. Long after I could read for myself, when my legs dangled to the floor, mother still took me on her lap and exposed me to wonderful books, including Bible stories. She never seemed to tire of reading to me. How I loved that! By reading to me mother instilled in me her love for books. Mother is eighty-six, has lived with us for sixteen years, and continues to be an avid reader. As I listen to young people today tell about the lack of love they have in their homes, I feel so very privileged to have been reared in a home with a mother and dad who loved me and really cared about me.

As a teen-ager, I attended young people's meetings, missionary meetings, and institutes for young people. I joined church and was baptized (sprinkled). In one meeting I went forward and dedicated my life (to whom I do not know) to become a nurse. I was an idealist, and as I watched some of my friends go forward, I thought this was a great idea so I joined them. I had many girl friends and boy friends and I loved them all. I was always the "big-sister" type and was constantly trying to help my friends with their problems. While a freshman in high school, I fell madly in love with a young man with whom I'm still madly in love today. That man is my husband. He shared with me his desire to become a doctor. Since we felt marriage was ultimately for us, the logical thing for me to do was to become a nurse. Since I knew my parents could not afford to send me through nurses' training, I was constantly looking for some other way. One day I spotted on the school's bulletin board the announcement of a statewide essay contest. Those who entered were to write one hundred words on "Why we thought a certain cap and gown were no better than the best, but better than the rest." Immediately I entered the contest. How excited my dad was the night I returned from a meeting and found him holding a letter in his hands. Guess what? I had won first prize. One hundred dollars! Was I thrilled! Now I knew I was going into nurses' training and that one hundred dollars did it. I took my training in a huge city hospital and loved it. Here again as I look back, I feel God had his hand on me and was preparing me for my future life.

Some day I may write a book on all the details

of my life because it truly has been an exciting and adventuresome one, but for now I'm anxious to get on to that special time in my life when I met the greatest friend I'll ever have.

Jack and I were married in 1940. He had just entered medical school and I had just graduated from nurses' training. During the first years of our marriage I did supervisory nursing in the hospital, several years of public health nursing, and private duty nursing. After my husband had an M.D. behind his name, and being more in love than ever, we decided it was time to start a family.

When our children were small (we have a family of four), we decided very nobly we would *take* our children to Sunday school. None of this "dropping them off and picking them up later" stuff for us. A regular trek to church on Sunday was a new phase of our lives. During the time I was in nurses' training I went to church only when a friend would invite me to go and that wasn't very often. After Jack and I were married, we went when we felt like it. After all, Sunday was the only day we had to "sleep in" and, really now, we needed this rest if we were to serve our fellowmen. How noble can one get!

By now, we had lived in several large cities. In one of these cities we were attending a downtown church. The lovely women of this church got their heads together and decided it was high time that a certain young married woman become involved in the "church work." I was that woman and, believe me, I did get involved. I became so involved I didn't know whether I was "pitchin" or "catchin." The more I did, the more I was asked to do. I took great pride in doing everything beautifully—for whom? I did these things for those dear women and also for myself and for what it did for my own ego. I not only used every available moment I could squeeze in, but I branched out in my involvement and did for others! Please don't misunderstand at this point. Doing for others and doing church work for God's glory is completely different than doing these things for oneself. Ego inflation I call it. My old ego would soar to about 100 percent when Mrs. Jones or Mrs. Smith would say, "Oh, you don't mean this pie is for us. You mean you took time out of your very busy day to do this for us?" Those words were music to my ears. I would go home and think, "Yes, I am good, I really am." I was good all right, but "good for nothing." I would think, "I will go to heaven because of all these good things I'm doing."

Little was I aware of how time was going to change all this.

CHAPTER II

"DOWN"— INTO THE VALLEY

*"I went down to the bottoms of the moun-
tains; the earth with her bars was about me
for ever: yet hast thou brought up my life
from corruption, O Lord my God."*
—Jonah 2:6

In the midst of all of my "do-gooding" a little incident happened between my husband and me re-
garding our older son, David. It completely shattered me and brought me to my knees. The tears
flowed and then I cried out to God, "Help me,
God, oh, please help me." Our David was a very
precocious, active youngster but we expected much
from him. If his performance was not up to our
expectations, my husband and I were disappointed.

Our Lord God works in such natural and logical
ways that many times we just cannot see his working. We have to have our eyes opened by him.

God works with each person differently. The
method he employed in my life to bring me to
himself probably will be completely different from
the way he brought you or will bring you. Remember God is unique; his methods are unique.

At this time God brought a young woman to our

house to work with me on a particular committee. In the course of our conversation she began telling me about some of the problems they were having with their daughter. She stated that they were receiving excellent help through the Child Guidance Center. I began to listen! Hm, I thought, maybe that's what we need to do—seek outside help. That night I broached the subject to my husband, I knew he was going to say no, but to my utter surprise he agreed. We took David to the clinic. They interviewed us separately and found our young son to be a normal, healthy boy, but they would like to continue to work with us. Was that ever a blow to our egos! We were into the whole thing now; there was nothing else to do but go on with it. I had even a bigger blow coming. After several months of counseling, each of us with a different person, they asked me if I could come twice a week instead of once. That was a bitter "pride" pill to swallow I'll tell you, but I condescended. Suddenly, as I was pouring out all my little petty problems to this good looking young man behind the desk, I realized how utterly negative I was about everything. I found I was beginning to confess some of my faults to him. One day he asked if he might tape our conversations. I consented. Thinking about it later, I was horrified at what I had done, but I don't mind now. Those tapes have all been wiped clean by Jesus.

On Sunday morning during this period of counseling at the clinic I didn't go to church. I was standing at the sink washing dishes, listening to the radio. Suddenly I was listening intently to an announcement about a new book. For no apparent reason I became excited, very excited about this book. I could hardly wait until the next morning to go to town to buy it. This book was the beginning of a long climb up the mountain that would eventually bring me out of the valley of darkness into the light, into vision. The whole thrust of the book was that there is power in thinking positively.

As I read the author's thoughts on positive thinking, again I realized how negative I was. If I had to catch a bus at the corner, before I even walked out my front door I knew I had missed that bus. I was also a "worry wart." I worried about anything and everything. This book was excellent and just what I needed at that time. In the book it stated that if one wanted peace of mind to do the following: First, ask God to reveal your sins to you and each day write one of your sins on a piece of paper. Second, ask God to forgive you of that sin and to erase it from your memory. Last, literally burn the paper. I took these instructions seriously since I wanted peace of mind. Each morning found me asking, writing, and burning. I often wondered as I stood at my kitchen sink burning that small scrap of paper what my neighbor would think if she suddenly appeared on the scene and saw what I was doing. However, that thought didn't deter me. I continued the ritual each day for several weeks. By this time my husband had completed his surgical residency in Wichita, Kansas and we were looking for a permanent location. Where to now??

CHAPTER III

"UP"—INTO VISION

*"Then spake Jesus again unto them, saying,
I am the light of the world: he that follow-
eth me shall not walk in darkness, but shall
have the light of life"*
—John 8:12

It all happened rapidly. The next thing we knew we were moving into the home of our children's dreams. They had made a list of things they would like in our new home. Lots of room, trees, fireplace. I'll never forget the excitement each of us experienced when we moved into that home on Lewis Avenue in Waukegan, Illinois. That home is a memorable one for me.

Soon after we were settled in our home and my husband had become a part of a group practice, I was invited by one of the doctor's wives to her home for tea. It was a very enjoyable afternoon. In the course of our conversation she remarked that she had just bought a new book. Since I had told her how I loved to read, she just knew I would like this book. As she took it from her bookshelf and handed it to me, I saw and felt its newness. I knew she hadn't even opened it. This seemed strange, offering me a book she hadn't read. But I thanked her for her thoughtfulness and left with *the book* in my hands. What a book! A newly published one, *A Man Called Peter,* by Catherine Marshall. Oh, how God used it in my life!

I began reading it the minute I arrived home and continued every time I had a free moment. Then came that night for me to forever remember. It was a cool, late October evening, the kind of night you like to curl up on your bed and read a good book. After my husband left for his nightly hospital rounds and I had the children tucked snugly in their beds, I grabbed my book, *A Man Called Peter,* curled up on the bed, and began reading. I have to be careful here how I state this or I might repeat what I said to one of the Christian Women's Clubs one night as I was relating my experience. I said, "I curled up on the bed with *A Man Called Peter.*" Such howls and I was astonished. What had I said? It suddenly dawned upon me what had come out of my mouth. I quickly explained what I meant and went on with my story. On the way home that night I asked the Lord why he had allowed me to say that because I reminded him that I had asked him to put every word on my lips he wanted me to say, and he whispered into my ear, "Someone needed to laugh at that very moment." That answer was good enough for me.

To continue, I was deeply engrossed in this marvelous book when I came to the part where Catherine Marshall was thinking, "I wonder what I would do if Jesus suddenly appeared at the foot of my bed." (If you have read the book, you will remember that Catherine Marshall had been ill for months and had not been out of bed for a long time.) She went on to say that just then Jesus did appear at the foot of her bed and spoke to her, saying, "Get up and go and tell your parents (her parents were sleeping in a room down the hall) you are going to be all right." She thought, I can't do it. Then she wondered if Jesus would ever give her another opportunity. If you haven't read the book I hope this will challenge you to read it.

After having read Catherine Marshall's words, I laid the book down and said aloud, "Lord, I want you to come into my heart and into my life and take over completely; I want you to be the Lord of my life." Now the cleansing process had been completed. I had been confessing and being cleansed for months. Our Lord took me at my word. In that moment he came into my heart and life and took over! Our bedroom lighted up as if thousands of 100-watt bulbs had been turned on. I knew he was there! I felt the presence of the living God! I knew I had found him. My search had been fruitful! I wanted to go up on the housetop and shout, "I've found the answer. I've found the answer to everything. Jesus—He is the answer!" I was completely filled with joy; I was bubbling on the inside. I read no more that night as I was too excited and happy and, oh, the peace I experienced—peace of mind and soul.

While my husband was preparing for bed I tried to share this wonderful experience with him. After he got into bed I said, "Honey, have you ever experienced anything like this?" He was well on his way to dreamland and mumbled something like, "Oh, I guess so once when I was overseas."

Needless to say, I didn't sleep a wink that night. I could hardly lie in bed, let alone sleep. I wish words would adequately express my feelings. I was thrilled. I was excited. I wanted to talk. I wanted to talk about him—Jesus. I knew now that he is a *real* person. Suddenly all I had ever heard about him came to my mind. I had *heard* he had died on the cross and shed his blood for the sins of the world. Now I *knew* he died on the cross and shed his blood—yes, for everyone in the world, even me. Now I had definite assurance that when I died I was going to be with him, I was going to heaven, and I was going to live forever! Oh, what peace that truth gave me! I wanted to jump up and down and shout but I didn't. I just lay in that bed and bathed myself in the luxury of it all. My thoughts continued, he is real, now I know he is real. He's here with me.

Now, nineteen years later he's still just as real as he was then. I'm still just as excited, just as thrilled as I was then, even more so! My eyes had been opened! Later when I began to read the Bible and came across the verse "Ye shall know the truth and the truth shall make you free" (John 8:32), I knew this was what had happened to me. I had to go down into the valley of despair and realize I had done, said, and thought wrong things. I was a sinner. There is just no other word for it. The Bible says in Romans 3:23, "For all have sinned, and come short of the glory of God." Yes, that was I, down into that valley, down to the end of myself, not knowing which way to turn, *but* I called for help. I called to God who took my hand and helped me up onto higher ground. He showed me the way up out of that valley and that way was Jesus Christ. The Bible states, "I am the way, the truth, and the life: no man cometh unto the Father, but by me" (John 14:6). I was cleansed because I had confessed. He says in 1 John 1:9 "If we confess our sins, he is faithful and just to forgive us our sins, and to cleanse us from all unrighteousness." I now had vision! I could see. My spiritual eyes were opened. Yes, I found my sight in the valley, *my* valley, no, *"the* Valley of Vision" (Isaiah 22:5). That little word *the* swings the door open to everyone, to whosoever will accept Jesus the Christ into his heart and life.

CHAPTER IV

SPIRITUALLY "BLIND—NOW I SEE"

"One thing I know, that, whereas I was blind, now I see"
—John 9:25

I jumped out of bed the next morning refreshed, excited, and exhilarated, even though I hadn't slept. We were planning a weekend trip to Fort Wayne, Indiana to visit some dear friends who had been our former neighbors. It was so difficult to keep quiet on that trip, but I did.

After we arrived at our friends' home, it was a different story. I followed her from room to room, from stove to table, and back again trying to relate to her my experience of the night before. She was very kind and gracious and listened attentively but I could tell by her facial expressions it all sounded very strange to her.

Back home once again, I still had an intense desire to share this experience with someone who perhaps could identify with me, having had a similar experience. Finally I decided our minister was the logical person. I called and made an appointment with him. As I entered his office and sat opposite him, I was happy, bubbling with joy, and extremely anxious to share my marvelous experience.

I began, reiterating each little detail, and the excitement within me grew greater and greater until I came to the tremendous climax, my encounter with Christ. I felt like a huge bubble about to burst. I stopped talking, waiting for the reaction I expected, but it didn't come. By this time our minister had pushed his glasses downward on his nose and was peering at me through the lower part of the glasses with bewilderment written all over his face. At last the words came, long and drawn out. "Mrs. Patterson, I have never heard anything like this before in my entire life." Oh, what a let down! I felt just like someone had taken a huge pin and burst the bubble. I went home deflated. Then the old devil saw his chance. He tried to tell me I hadn't had an experience, that I *wasn't* changed, and on and on. I knew I was different; I was thinking differently, my attitudes were changed, and I had a terrific desire to read the Bible—that I knew was different.

In the mornings after the children left for school, I would grab my Bible, sit in our little breakfast nook and begin to read. A few days after visiting our minister, I was alone in the breakfast nook reading in the third chapter of John where Nicodemus had gone to Jesus and asked him how he could get to heaven. I came to the verse where Jesus told Nicodemus, "You must be born again."

I began to ask God, "What has happened to me?

I know something very definitely has, but what is
it? God, I have to know!" I reread the words that
Jesus spoke to Nicodemus, "You must be born
again." It suddenly hit me like a ton of bricks.
That's it, why, of course, that's it. I've been born a
second time. The picture was very clear before
me! My obstetrical experience in nurse's training
came into focus. I saw at once the thumbnail
sketch Jesus made for Nicodemus. The physical
birth—Jesus said, a man must be born of water.
Now I saw it, the baby being ushered into the
world through the flesh, the mother's birth canal;
then one must be born of the Spirit, the *spiritual
birth*. Jesus said, "That which is born of the flesh is
flesh; and that which is born of the Spirit is spirit"
(John 3:6).

It all jelled! I cried out, "That's what has happened to me; I've been born spiritually; I've been
born again!" Oh, what a thrill! God had answered.
He had made very clear exactly what had taken
place in my life. "Oh, thank you, thank you, God."
I was very quiet for a few moments, wishing I had
someone to talk to about God, someone who knew
what I was talking about, someone who understood. Suddenly I was asking, "Please, Lord, send
me a friend who can talk to me, who will understand; someone who is excited about this second
birth I've just experienced, this spiritual birth.
Thank you." God is full of the unexpected. At that
very moment he was preparing a wonderful surprise for me.

CHAPTER V

"A SURPRISE AND A DREAM"

*"Draw nigh to God, and He will draw nigh
to you"*

—James 4:8

*"The Lord is nigh unto all them that call
upon Him, to all that call upon Him in
truth"*

—Psalm 145:18

I was up to my ears in fruitcakes the afternoon
God delivered my surprise and the answer to my
prayer. Fruitcake baking for Christmas gifts and
selling had become a ritual in my kitchen, starting
sometimes as early as the week after Thanksgiving. This had all begun when we lived in Wichita,
Kansas. Lottie, a close friend of mine, had given
this very special recipe to me. The cake always
turned out great regardless of how I put it together, and lovers of fruitcake seemed to think it the
"best ever." That's when I got the idea of baking
them to sell. I always hated the idea of buying my
husband's gift with money he had earned and given
to me. I knew full well it was still his money that
bought the ingredients for the cakes, but I spent
the time preparing and selling them. Consequent-

ly, I felt his gift from me was a little more *from* me.

If you should happen to stop by to see me two to three weeks before Christmas, you no doubt would smell that delectable aroma of fruitcake coming from my oven. Funny thing, not one member of our family likes fruitcake (not even mine), but if I just barely mention that I might not bake fruitcake this year, I hear the laments of "Oh, mom, no, you can't stop that." Fruitcake baking has become a tradition, and our family loves the little things we have done over and over that are just peculiar to our family. No doubt your family is the same. You just had to know about the fruitcake because again it demonstrates how God works through natural ways to bring about the answers to prayers. I have also experienced God's *supernatural* power, so I'm not discounting that. We cannot limit God!

I was hurrying to get the last cake in the oven before the children came from school when the phone rang. A very pleasant and enthusiastic voice said, "Mrs. Patterson, you haven't met me. I'm Beulah Kucera and I understand you make and sell fruitcakes. I'm wondering if I might buy several as I enjoy giving them as Christmas gifts." I assured her I had cakes to sell.

She continued talking but all I heard was . . . "in my Christian life." "Are you a Christian?" I asked. She replied, "Yes, I am." I returned, "A born-again Christian?" "Yes, I am." Then in a pleading voice I said, "Would you have time to talk to me about the Lord? Perhaps I could deliver your cakes at a time when you would have time to talk." Then came the surprise. "Well," she said. "You wouldn't have very far to go since we live right across the street from you."

Putting down the phone, I said, "Thank you, Lord, you are full of wonderful surprises." Perhaps you are questioning how this could happen. She lived across the street from me and I didn't know her. We had lived in this home only a few months. Thinking back, I remember we had only lived in our new home a few days when I heard that the woman living across the street had died. Mrs. Kucera told me that this couple and she and her husband attended the same church. Beulah and Dolph had moved in with their friend to help him adjust to his situation and to comfort and care for him for a few months.

On Saturday afternoon I had some free time. I decided to rest awhile and then deliver the fruitcakes. I didn't intend to go to sleep but I did and had a dream that was very real. In the dream I was with a group of people sitting in a circle. A man holding onto a woman's hand came up to me and said, "I will lead you and she will feed you." Then I was awake. The words kept repeating themselves in my mind, "I will lead you and she will feed you." I knew it had to be Jesus that I had seen in the dream and I just felt the woman had to be Mrs. Kucera. I was ringing her doorbell in no time flat.

We took care of the business of the cakes, exchanged pleasantries, and then began talking about the Lord. She told me of her conversion, about the joy she was experiencing teaching a Sunday school class, and then she added she had just taken on a new job of selling Christian books. I couldn't wait any longer, I had to share my dream with her. I told her I felt she was the woman that Jesus had told me would feed me because I didn't know any other Christian women in town. She said she would do her best to help me grow in the Christian life and began her task that very moment by placing a Christian book in my hands. Here again I thank God for Beulah Kucera and the love he has given me for books. At first she gave me one; then two at a time. I returned them so rapidly she began giving me five at a time. I look back and wonder how I managed my time. I had four children, a big house to keep clean, cooking, and such. I also kept my "time alone" with the Lord each morning because reading the Bible and prayer always came first.

Beulah also introduced me to radio station WMBI. The people at that station, Moody Bible Institute, became my constant companions. I soon learned they offered Bible correspondence courses. I decided to try one. Why not? I sincerely wanted to learn what God had to say to me; therefore, I began another wonderful adventure in learning. Mothers, if life seems to be dull and you realize you aren't using that gray matter up there in your brain that God gave you, why not take a Bible correspondence course?

Before leaving this chapter, I would like to present to Beulah, my adopted spiritual mother, a beautiful spiritual bouquet. A bouquet in the form of God's own words in Philippians 1:2-3. "Grace be unto you, and peace, from God our Father, and from the Lord Jesus Christ. I thank my God upon every remembrance of you." She was never too busy to talk to me. When I called, she always gave me the required spiritual vitamins and pointed me to verses in the Bible that would comfort, encourage, give me peace, teach, or whatever was necessary at the time. I was such an eager student that same days I called her as many as eight times. She never tired of me or my enthusiasm for God.

I do hope this chapter will stimulate other Christians to be on their toes, aware of anyone who might be crying out to be fed spiritually. Give them of yourself and time until they can, at least, crawl or begin to walk on their own. Too many Christians are guilty of leading someone to the Lord Jesus and then walking away. They leave him dangling without knowing anything about the source of food, the Bible, to help him grow in this new style of life.

Also I say a loud amen for sound Christian books! I know God used them and is continuing to use them in my life to help me grow spiritually. I *never* put Christian books ahead of the Bible, but education in any area is a continuing process and we can truly grow and learn from one another.

Yes, our Father used two natural means, a surprise and a dream, to launch me onto the pathway to spiritual maturity.

CHAPTER VI

WITNESSING:
"THE LOST AND FOUND DEPARTMENT"

"Go ye into all the world, and preach the gospel to every creature"
—Mark 16:15

"For this my son was dead, and is alive again; he was lost, *and is* found*"*
—Luke 15:24

As I was meditating, that still, small voice spoke to me saying he would like me to dedicate this chapter to my brother Paul. Immediately my thoughts were taken back many years ago when God found Paul and set him upon the solid rock, Christ Jesus. "No man can come to me, except the Father which hath sent me draw him: and I will raise him up at the last day" (John 6:44). Several years later when God first began nudging me to write, I shared this nudging with Paul. I suggested perhaps we could write a book together, but to him it seemed impossible, as he was in Texas and I was living at that time in Illinois. He said perhaps some day he might write one and if he did, he would call it *Lost and Found*. I never questioned him as to where he got his title but as I was thinking and reading again about the prodigal son in Luke 15:24, I wondered, could that have been his source? I'm using this scripture to emphasize my chapter heading but I didn't steal it from big brother! The title for this chapter came straight from the Holy Spirit in answer to prayer. This is how it happened.

I had been asked to conduct a mini session on witnessing at the Win-some Women's Retreat at Winona Lake, Indiana. Ethel Anderson, their capable and efficient chairman, had asked me to get a quick note off to her immediately giving my session a "catchy" name. Driving home from a meeting that afternoon, I prayed, "Oh, Holy Spirit God, please give me a catchy name for that mini session on witnessing. Please give it to me soon, as Ethel wants it immediately." I no sooner breathed that prayer when the words came just like this: "Witnessing: the Lost and Found Department." "Oh, thank you God for giving it to me quickly." This title *was* used for the mini session. Shortly thereafter I decided to use this same title for this chapter. Paul, the following words are lovingly dedicated to you.

Many Christians do not witness. I mean actually

confess Christ with their mouths. I'm afraid too many hide behind the words "actions speak louder than words." I've seen many people who do not know Christ personally display some beautiful and lovely actions, but Jesus said we must "confess him before men if he is to confess us before the Father." I think that's a rather stiff admonition to his sons and daughters. How many Christians do you know who seemingly are unaware of that verse? I haven't been able to keep my mouth shut about him—the one who has done so much for me. On the other hand there are others who *never* open their mouths. I have asked myself over and over—why? I have come to the conclusion that Christians who do not share Christ with others are not filled with the Holy Spirit. When one is filled to overflowing with his spirit, he has what some call *holy boldness*—and that's just what it is. Whenever the opportunity presents itself we find ourselves speaking out. The Lord has taught me not to force him upon anyone. If I'm "on my toes" and looking and listening I find opportunities everywhere I turn. I do not make opportunities or open doors to him unless I'm specifically directed to do so by the Holy Spirit. Of course, there may be some who disagree with this viewpoint and I'm sure there are exceptions because there are usually exceptions to all rules.

If you are blessed with this holy boldness, then, in addition, you should have some authority behind you and, of course, our authority in witnessing is God's word, the Bible. It's not always convenient to have your Bible with you; consequently, it is important to have some verses memorized. God admonishes each of us to "hide his Word in our hearts." It not only helps in witnessing but also edifies oneself. Memorizing Scripture is a great brain exerciser. Try it and you will find out. If a verse of Scripture has meant something special to me, it is easier for me to memorize. Perhaps some of you have stopped memorizing. I challenge you today to begin again! If we have memorized God's word, the Holy Spirit will bring it quickly to our attention just at the precise moment we need it. The more you memorize, the easier it becomes.

I heard a simple method given one time that *anyone* can use in witnessing. You need to know only three verses of Scripture. You tell the person to whom you are witnessing that to accept Christ, to know him personally, and to receive the marvelous gift of eternal life is as easy as ABC. Accept, believe, and confess.

A. Accept. Ask Jesus to come into your heart and life and take over completely. Jesus says in Revelation 3:20, "Behold, I stand at the door, and knock: if any man hear my voice, and open the door. I will come in to him, and will sup with him, and he with me."

B. Believe. If you have asked him to come in, then believe he has done just what you have asked him to do. "Believe on the Lord Jesus Christ, and thou shalt be saved" (Acts 16:31).

C. Confess, admit that you are a sinner. There's not one of us who would have to think back very far to realize we have sinned, but Jesus says in 1 John 1:9, "If we confess our sins, he is faithful and just to forgive us our sins, and to cleanse us from all unrighteousness." Don't you agree? Isn't this a very simple and painless way in presenting the plan by which a person can know Christ and inherit the kingdom of heaven?

If someone with a beautifully wrapped gift in his hand came to your door today and said, "It's for you, all you have to do is take it," how many seconds would it take for you to accept it. Not many. Then *why* does it take so long for us to make up our minds about Christ and the wonderful gift of living forever with him? *Eternity* . . . have you ever thought a moment on that word? It's forever and ever and ever. We just cannot comprehend its full meaning with our finite minds. Perhaps, dear one, as you are reading this, you cannot recall ever making a definite decision for Christ. Perhaps you have sat in a church for years, professing to be a Christian (as I did). You think you are going to heaven but you aren't sure. Don't wait any longer. Stop reading right now because God is speaking to you. Confess your sins. Ask him to come into your life and take over. Believe he has done what you've asked and thank him. Now you know you are going to heaven because John 1:12 says, "But as many as received him, to them gave he power to become the sons of God, even to them that believe on his name."

Our approach in witnessing is of great importance. An overzealous person may rush up to someone, slap him on the back and say crudely, "Sister—or brother—are you saved?" We cannot say God never uses this method because we cannot limit God. He can use anyone or any method to do his work in spite of the person or the method used, but it just doesn't appear to be the "norm" in witnessing. When we witness we go in faith. Where there is faith there is love, a loving concern for the other person. An understanding heart is also of prime importance.

There are many ways 'direct and indirect' in which we can witness. In your correspondence it's always easy and acceptable to write out a Scripture verse. At the end of your letter you can refer to it as a verse that had meant much to you and you wanted to share it. One lady writes a verse of Scripture on the stubs of her bills that she sends with her check payments. Why not try it? The giving of Christian books is an easy and rewarding way to witness because everyone gets something from each book he reads. When you give, don't say you are giving it because you think he needs it. Give it in love, sharing with him what the book has meant to you. I ask God to direct me as to what book I should give since each person's reaction is different. You may think a certain book is terrific, but the next person may not care for it. The giving of Christian books as gifts is a way in which you can use your love-offering money. The love-offering money is that money you give over and above your tithe. Some people feel free to use their tithe money for books. I'm sure God blesses them for it. You women who have telephonitis (I understand this is a disease not common to *men*, only women) use every opportunity to witness on the phone. When someone calls and asks you to pray about such and such, don't say "I will," but say "I'll pray right now over the phone." The person on the other end of the line may not be a Christian but your love for him, demonstrated in this manner, may be just the open door for you.

Let's take a look at how to witness to our loved ones and to our own household. I have found from my own experience that it is always acceptable to share with our loved ones incidents in which God has played a part that would be *interesting to them*. Do not preach. Preaching to our loved ones tends to close more doors than it opens. Sharing, yes; preaching, no. God just simply didn't or couldn't work in my loved ones' lives until I committed them into his hands and permitted him to work with them. You may be saying, "Now what does she mean? Commit him or her into God's hands?" It means exactly this: Whatever or whoever it might be, you just simply say: "Father, here they are. I've done all I can do. I'm turning them over to you. Thank you for what you are going to do." Then leave them with him.

One morning the Lord gave me this simple method in which to do this committing. Since women like action, the Lord told me to write my request on a piece of paper, to get that unused sugar bowl down from the top shelf of my cabinet. Please dump out the sugar. Ours are always full. Grandma sees to that, place my request inside the bowl, put on the lid, put it back on the shelf, and say, "There it is, Lord. You may have it." Try this method of committal. He will honor it. If at any time in the future you are tempted to take it to the Lord again, stop and say, "Lord, you have it. Thank you for what you are doing."

Another way to witness is to sing about him as you go about your home doing the daily chores. It will make you as well as others happy. One thing I would definitely like to stress; have a devotional time each day with your family. If your husband hasn't assumed his rightful role in this, then you must do it. Train those children in God's ways.

Witness at work. I'm a registered nurse and I work for my surgeon husband. Whenever God gives me an opportunity, I witness for him. The other day I prayed with a woman over a problem that loomed huge in her world. She told me at a later visit that I wouldn't believe all that had happened to them since that prayer. She said she and her husband had drifted away from the Lord and my praying for her (I think I shocked her) had made her aware of the fact. Catherine, our secretary, puts little devotional books on our tables in the waiting room. This is a definite witness. People do read them.

Some are seed sowers and some reap the harvest. A Scripture that has been a great comfort to me is Psalms 126:5-6. "They that sow in tears shall reap in joy. He that goeth forth and weepeth, bearing precious seed, shall doubtless come again with rejoicing, bringing his sheaves with him." If you are like me, many times you have witnessed to someone and then shed tears, believing you had messed up the whole thing. When we have witnessed to someone in sincerity, we should just leave the results with God. His Holy Spirit will take what we have said and use it. God has said: "So shall my word be that goeth forth out of my mouth: it shall not return unto me void, but it shall accomplish that which I please, and it shall prosper in the thing whereto I sent it" (Isaiah 55:11). If possible, we should always sprinkle God's words along with our own. All God wants from us is to be faithful to him in witnessing to all he puts in our way.

A marvelous witness for your home is placing a picture of Christ in a spot where it can be seen from your front door. One of the first things our Becky did when we moved into our home in Fort Wayne was to place a large picture of Christ over a table in our foyer where it can be seen from the door. It probably has been more of a witness than we will ever realize.

How about starting a Bible study in your neighborhood? Send out invitations to all your neighbors. Then ask God to send those of his choice. I'll never forget the first Bible study group I started here in our neighborhood. On the day we completed the last lesson, one of my closest friends now got to her feet and told her story. She had been reared in one church. After her marriage she became a member of another church for her husband's sake and up to this time had held many positions in the church. As she progressed with this course, reading the Scriptures, she began to see that she really wasn't a Christian. Another neighbor also became a Christian from taking that course. If you can't lead a group or be a part of a group, take a course by yourself. You will find it very rewarding.

God is bidding us go forth with his precious seed, the "good news," that those who are *lost* can be *found*. *You* are *his* mouthpiece in the lost and found department. Begin today to serve him with your mouth!

CHAPTER VII

"SPIRITUAL HORS D'OEUVRES"

*"One generation shall praise thy works to
another, and shall declare thy mighty acts"*
—Psalm 145:4

*"Gather up the fragments that remain, that
nothing be lost"*

—John 6:12

This book has actually been in the process of being
written for many years. I have notes on little
scraps of paper, some in a big notebook, some in a
small notebook. As I've written, I've gathered up
one thought from here, another experience from
there. In essence, this book is a gathering together
of the fragments that remain. These fragments put
together tell of my walk with Jesus these past
twenty years. I had a definite confirmation of this
fact this week from a dear friend of only a few
years, Norma Browning. She took time out to
write to me knowing I was here in Wisconsin writing "the book." She shared the John 6:12 verse
with me and told me the Lord had given it to *her*
that morning. She thought perhaps she should
share it as she felt it might also have a message for
me. She said, "Maybe, Betsy, you are to gather up

the fragments of your thoughts and experiences that they might be passed on to others and not be lost."

This definitely had been my idea as I wrote notes concerning my thoughts and experiences over the past years, saving them that I might share them with others. I have felt since I've been here and during the time I was writing each day that the Holy Spirit was saying, "There are to be twelve chapters in our book." As I was rereading John 6:12 this morning and was closing the Bible, the Spirit said, "Read the next verse." As I read verse 13 chills went all over me. Jesus went on to say to his disciples, "Therefore they gathered them together, and filled *twelve baskets with the fragments* of the five barley loaves, which remained over and above unto them that had eaten." Again my confirmation for the *twelve* chapters. They gathered those fragments together into twelve baskets. Before I leave John 6:12, I wish to pass on to you the message *Norma* received from the Lord on this. Perhaps you "savers" will be comforted anew. Norma reminded me what a saver she is. As she saved each and every little thing she began to wonder if she might not be a little silly about it. Then she read John 6:12 in her morning devotions. She ended by saying, "Could this be my gift?" to be able to see uses for things which would otherwise be lost. So take heart, savers, this verse *has* to be for you. Feel free to go right on and save those bottles, jars, string!

You have already had a taste of my spiritual hors d'oeuvres but now let's pass the tray around again. "Taste and see if the Lord is good." I see so many tasty tidbits it's a task to know just those that you will prefer. Here again I'm leaning hard on the Holy Spirit. Here's one I would like you to taste; it fits perfectly in this spot. I thought of it as I read of the multiplication of the loaves and fishes. I had a similar experience of multiplication. God is the same today as he was yesterday. He can still multiply our substance if need be. I know he can. He did it for me.

I write from my notes written many years ago so it will be written for you just as it happened. Remember my fruitcake business? I was in the process of finishing up the cakes and had ingredients for only several more when a lady from our church called and asked if the church might buy some of my cakes for Christmas gifts to give to our shut-ins. She stated she would like to have twelve small cakes and she had the money to pay for them. I assured her I would love to supply the cakes! Leaving the phone I knew I would not take a penny for them. I also knew one recipe made two small cakes. As I viewed my materials, I had only enough for three recipes or six small cakes and I didn't have money to buy any more ingredients. What to do? I didn't even consider what I would do. I just began preparing the cakes, each recipe put together in a separate mixing bowl. I had six pans prepared to receive the batter from the three recipes. I poured the batter from the first bowl into the first pan, then went on to the next. I noticed I had the second pan almost full and there seemed to be enough for another. I went to the third pan. After filling that one, there was still more, so I filled the fourth pan. I looked at those four pans full of batter with puzzlement and quickly picked up the second bowl. After filling two pans, I had to stop and prepare more pans. I filled two more pans from that bowl. Very excited and trembling, I began to spoon the batter from the last bowl. I had to stop and prepare *more* pans. Yes, you have guessed it. When I finished I had twelve small pans filled with fruitcake batter and I was only supposed to have six. My husband had helped me prepare these cakes many times. In fact one year he helped me make one hundred twelve pounds, so I know he was familiar with the cakes and knew one recipe yielded two small ones. I ran to the stairway and called to him, as he was upstairs. "Honey, come down here and see what the Lord has done." I find tears of gratitude coming to my eyes in just the remembering of this miracle. He looked at the three bowls and then at the twelve cakes in utter amazement! Thus, God provided the fruitcakes for the shut-ins without my purchasing more ingredients for them. Nothing is impossible with God.

Here comes the tray again loaded with those goodies. How about seconds? One cold and wintry night deep snow covered the streets of Waukegan.

Jack and I were "snug as bugs in a rug" in our chairs before our huge fireplace deeply engrossed in reading. Unexpectedly my husband got up from his chair, went into the foyer, and looked out through the small window at the top of the door. He turned to me and said, "Honey, there's a car stuck in the snow across the street and I believe it's Dolph. He's trying to get it out." With no further ado he put on his coat, hat, and gloves and called to me over his shoulder, "I'm going to see if I can help him." As the door closed quietly behind him, the phone in the kitchen rang. It was Beulah, Dolph's wife. In a quiet but excited voice, she said, "Betts, I'm praising God. I was greatly concerned about Dolph trying to get our car out of that snowbank. Seeing a light in your living room, I fell to my knees and asked God if he would somehow get a message to Jack to come and help Dolph." Oh, such a simple request but God put the message on his direct wire to Jack. "Before they call, I will answer; and while they are yet speaking, I will hear" (Isaiah 65:24). She continued, "I got up from my knees, went to the front window, and saw Jack crossing the street headed for Dolph." I can still hear her saying, "Isn't God good, Betts?" I gave a loud "Amen." Psalm 34 says, "Blessed is the man that trusteth in Him." Oh, that Christians would trust him more! They are missing much by not doing so.

Some of you are still hungry, reaching out for another morsel of spiritual experience. I'm so grateful and thrilled that God revealed that he was interested in *every* detail of my life, no matter how insignificant it seemed to me.

I was ironing in our big sunny room over the garage. It was shortly after lunch and my husband was just leaving for the office. As he kissed me goodbye, he asked if I had any money. He needed $1.50 for a hair cut. I hesitated in answering as I well knew $1.50 was all I had in my purse until payday, which was two days away. I hated to relinquish it, but I gave it to him, saying nothing. After he left I began to murmur to God. Do you ever murmur to God? Murmuring is complaining and complaining is sin. I complained, "God, why did you let him take my last $1.50 and it's two days yet until I get my allowance." Then came the still small voice saying, "Have I ever failed you?" "No, Lord." "Then trust me for this." "All right, Lord, I'll trust you." I promptly forgot the money and finished the ironing.

I was at the kitchen sink washing the dishes that evening when the doorbell rang and I heard my husband go to the door. I couldn't hear the conversation, but in the next moment my husband was standing beside me at the sink. He said, "Hold out your hand, honey." I did and he place a one-dollar bill and a fifty-cent piece in my hand. "What's this all about?" "Here's the $1.50 you gave me this afternoon." Startled and puzzled I said, "Where did it come from?" With a rather impish look on his face he said, "The man you heard at the door just handed me a subpoena to appear in court tomorrow and he explained whenever they hand a subpoena to a doctor, they also give him $1.50. Now don't ask me why because I don't know." With that he walked from the room. Again I was amazed at God's love in the little things. With my hand still open, my gaze left the $1.50 and my eyes turned upward and I said, "Thank you, Lord."

More you say? All right, here's another tidbit. One evening I was among a group of women who were giving a dinner for our men's group at church. The church had just recently installed an electric dishwasher and I had never used it before. There was a note of warning above it about keeping hands out of it because of its extremely high temperature. We were busy talking and I forgot and thrust my right hand into the water. I knew I had scalded it; the pain was intense. I jerked it out quickly and another woman wrapped it in a cloth. After trying unsuccessfully to get my husband, they called another doctor who said he would meet me at the hospital. A friend volunteered to take me in her car. The pain continued to be excruciating and as I walked from the kitchen, I exchanged a glance with a dear prayer partner of mine! That glance said, "Pray for me." The returned glance said, "I will." Before we had driven a block the pain had completely subsided. While I was sitting waiting for the doctor I took the cloth from my hand and there was a perfectly normal hand. When the doctor came I told him about thrusting my hand into the scalding water. He said, "You wait until tomorrow. This hand will be nothing but blisters." He applied a salve and bandages. The next day my husband took the bandages off to dress it. My hand was just as normal as the other one. From that time until now whenever I have received a burn from my iron, stove, or oven, it has hurt for a second so that I know I have burned myself, but the burning sensation immediately leaves me. The burn might even leave a scar, but I never feel any pain after the initial slight burning sensation.

You might as well take another tidbit. It's just like the one you had before in the form of a "God-incident," not a coincidence. Angie was four months old and the doctor suggested I take her off the breast and give her just plain bottle milk. He had given me a prescription that would dry up the milk. I was discussing this with one of my friends. She said she hoped I wouldn't have the difficulty she experienced with the medication. It had dried up her milk but it had also made her so ill with nausea and vomiting that she had to be in bed. I said, "Lord, you know all about this. I'll just leave this whole thing in your hands." That night I decided I would feed our little one on the breast for the last time at six o'clock the next morning. When I nursed her at two o'clock in the morning, my breasts were full of milk and it was in every way a completely normal feeding.

At six o'clock in the morning I got her up for her

last breast feeding. To my astonishment, my breasts were completely flat, absolutely void of any milk. So it was that our little girl had already had her last breast feeding at two o'clock. My husband, wide-eyed with amazement, said nothing, went to the kitchen, warmed some plain milk, and we proceeded to give it to her from a cup. From then on she drank from a cup with absolutely no crying for the breast. Furthermore, I never took one dose of the prescription the doctor gave me for drying up the milk. Praise be to our wonderful heavenly Father!

CHAPTER VIII

A HERITAGE OF THE LORD

*"Lo, children are an heritage of the Lord;
and the fruit of the womb is his reward."*

—Psalm 127:3

I do not set myself up as an authority on how to "train up" your child, but I believe this book would not be complete if I omitted this chapter about children. My desire is only to share some of our experiences with you. We continue to have many experiences as our Angie is still at home with us. She is a lively fourteen-year-old, keeping our challenge ever before us to train her in the knowledge and admonition of the Lord. Proverbs 22:6 "Train up a child in the way he should go: and when he is old, he will not depart from it" (Proverbs 22:6). I wonder how many professing Christian mothers and fathers have taken this admonition seriously.

Sometime ago I was to speak to a Christian women's group in Ohio. Before I got to my feet a lovely woman shared a three-line quip with me. It goes like this: Young people today want to:

walk before they crawl,

teach before they learn,

retire before they work.

When I got home that night I shared this with Angie. She said nothing, but the next morning before leaving for school she said, "Mother, I want to add a last line to what you told me last night." "I'm all ears," I said. "Go ahead." "What about this, mother, for a last line? They want to die before they live." As I pass this on to you, I would like to qualify the above four lines. This is not true of all young people. It's only true of a small percentage of young people. These words describe perfectly some we see each day.

As I share some of my experiences with you, possibly you will glean an idea or two that will be helpful. If so, thank God, as he is my source. Six requisites I believe are necessary in developing a sense of responsibility in our children. These requisites are directed to Christian parents. If you are not a Christian or you are not sure you are a Christian, stop right now in your reading, turn to chapter six, and follow my directions on how to become a Christian.

When you are sure your child can understand, tell him in simple words how he can become a Christian. You will be able to tell by his reponse whether he is ready for this experience. If not, try again when he seems ready.

The six requisites are:

1. Be living examples before your children of what you want them to be.
2. Spend time each day with your children reading about, talking about, and talking to God
3. Each day spend at least fifteen minutes alone with each child doing only what he would like to do.
4. Have faith in your children showing them you are trusting them.
5. Encourage initiative in your children.
6. Love them both physically and mentally with an understanding heart.

Now let's take a look at each of these separately.

Number One. We must keep in close touch with the Lord if we are to be living examples of our children. They observe our attitudes and actions and listen to our words more than we would like to believe. If we lie in front of them, we sanction lying (if only a little white lie). If we are critical, they will become critical. If we scream, they will scream. If we curse, they will curse—yes, they will, maybe not before us but when they are with others. They have read us loud and clear when we have said, "Don't do as I do, do as I say." If we keep ourselves neat and clean, if our homes are well kept, and if we hang up our clothes, our children will take note. Mother says, "Hang up your coat, Susie. Susie, didn't I tell you to hang up your coat!" Do you recognize yourself? You've said it twice. Suddenly you remember you must put the meat on for dinner and you forget to say more to Susie. Then later on *you* hang up Susie's coat. It is better to go to Susie, and with love and firmness insist that she hang up her coat. After several times of doing this, she will obey as soon as you ask her. Carrying through on our commands is most important. I wish I had learned this as our boys were growing up. I was a good, broken record and our boys soon learned that. Insistence should have been executed. We are the living examples; our children are the imitators. If we set good examples in disciplining them, being consistent, and following through on our words to them, they will continue to imitate us as they live their lives and rear *their* children.

Number Two. Have a worship time with your children. The leader should be you, dad, but if you will not assume this role, then, mother, you had better take over. God has said, "My word . . . shall not return unto me void" (Isaiah 55:11). God will honor you for every minute you spend reading to your children about him, teaching them to pray from their hearts. They will be eternally grateful to you for this. Read the Bible to them and discuss what you have read, permitting them to participate. When they are older encourage them to have their own quiet time.

The time I spent with our children in this way did more for them than any other one thing I did. It has paid off in great dividends. I praise God. After I had shared with them everything I knew about God, the daily experiences I had with God, and explanations of Scripture, I had done all I knew to do. I was able, with complete freedom, to permit them to leave our home, to go away to school, turning them over or committing them into God's hands knowing he would continue the work he had begun in them.

Send your child off to school with a Bible verse. I used a promise box. You can buy them at any Christian bookstore. Let your children choose a card and read their own verse if they can; if not, read it to them. Then just before they go out the door have a short prayer with them. Think what a change this would be rather than screaming at them as they leave you. Kiss each one, put your hand on the shoulder of the older ones, squeeze the younger ones, show them you love them, tell them you know their day will go well. If each mother and child parted like this in the mornings, think what our schoolrooms would be like!

One time when my husband and I were away from home, grandma told me that when it came time for the school bus to pick Angie up, she went to the door with Angie to watch for it. Angie looked up at her and said, "Well, go on, grandma." Grandma answered, "What do you mean?" "I mean go on. Mother always prays for me before I leave." So grandma prayed with Angie. Later, when grandma told me about this she said, "It really pays off, doesn't it, if we are just faithful and set the example."

Number Three. Spend fifteen minutes alone with each child. It will do wonders for your children. "Try it, you'll like it." Just couldn't help but repeat that TV commercial. It fits so well here. In those fifteen to thirty minutes or any amount of time you can give to each child, permit him to choose what he would like to have you do with him. Perhaps he will want you to do unexpected things like being held on your lap or being rocked. Some like to read to you; others want you to read to them. Take a short walk together or just get down on the floor with the building blocks. You name it; they can think of it. Sometimes it's hard for them to believe you are going to spend a time alone with them. Brothers and sisters learn to respect this time because they know their time is coming. You can even take the phone off the hook (if there is no one else to answer it) to assure them this is their time. This idea was not original with me. I adopted it from the book, *New Ways to Discipline* by Dorothy Baruch. Another Christian book on the market that is excellent is *Dare to*

Discipline by Charles Dobson. Charlotte, our daughter-in-law, had requested some help in disciplining our grandsons, Davey and Robbie, and I had said something about it in our Bible study group. Bertie, a friend, suggested this book. I thanked her and intended to purchase it at my first opportunity. The next morning there was a package in our mailbox. The enclosed note stated it was just a little gift from the Christian School, given to us in appreciation. Praise God! I knew then and there it was the book the Lord wanted Charlotte to have. She says it's great and has helped her a lot. I say again, "Time alone with each child works wonders. *Try it, you all will like it.*"

Number Four. Have faith in your children. We all like to be trusted. As we trust our children they develop a sense of responsibility and a desire to be what they know we expect and trust them to be. Each time I left Becky at Interlochen, my last words to her were, "Honey, be as sweet as people think you are." As each child grew older we added to their responsibilities.

Mort, our second son, showed a real sense of responsibility at age sixteen. While driving our car, he was involved in a minor accident. Just prior to the accident he had received his first paycheck of one hundred dollars. He was so thrilled with it that he had the check cashed for one-hundred one-dollar bills. I can well remember the happiness he expressed as he showed me that huge roll of bills. He felt so wealthy. He tucked them away in a drawer and thought he was sitting on top of the world financially. Then came the blow. His dad explained to him that we would be responsible for the first one hundred dollars in the repair on the car. Without any further word, Mort went to the drawer where his precious one hundred dollars were tucked away, brought them out, and put them into his dad's hands. His dad accepted the money because by so doing he knew he was helping develop responsibility in Mort. It was indeed difficult for me to keep my lips closed. As I stood alone in the kitchen, tears flowing, I breathed a prayer for Mort. I knew what that money meant to him. I thank God daily that my husband had that kind of wisdom because this incident, along with many others, were stepping stones to the responsibilities Mort now assumes flying jets for the United States Air Force.

Number Five. Encourage initiative in your children. You can begin work on this one at an early age. Permit them to feed themselves as soon as they seem to have the inclination. Here is another example. I can see a little three-year-old girl pulling her chair over to the sink where mommy is washing dishes. She wants to wash dishes, too. Encourage her to watch you this time and then tell her you will let her try the next time. Be sure you carry through on your promise. Show her how, carefully handling each dish. Teach her how to dry each dish thoroughly, also the knives, forks, and spoons. Then let her go ahead alone. Don't stand over her; see how she does alone. Praise and encourage her. You can come back to her at intervals, perhaps suggesting and correcting in love, but don't forget the praise. This method can also apply to little boys in whatever they want to do to help either mother or daddy. Don't let "no" become a habit with you. Examine mentally what your child wants to do before answering *yes* or *no*.

Paper routes for boys tend to foster initiative and responsibility. Both our boys, David and Mort, had paper routes. They not only had to use their initiative at times but it also brought our family together. Sometimes it became a family project and took teamwork in bad weather to get those papers delivered.

Number Six. Love the children physically. Take time out to cuddle your little ones, put your arm around their shoulders. Kiss your child goodbye and take time to go to the door with him. Take time out to listen to their problems. Talk with them about whatever is bothering them. Pray with them. All of these add up to love.

If you have made a mistake in dealing with your child, do not hesitate to say you are sorry. If you say you are sorry, it will teach him to say he is sorry when he has made a mistake.

I found this method effective in disciplining our children. After the disciplinary measures were completed, I would have our child ask God to forgive him for being disobedient. Then he would tell me he was sorry for disobeying me. This brought God into the picture and also taught him to go to God when he had sinned. Before I let our children go from me I always loved them physically and told them I loved them. This establishes a wonderful rapport between parent and child.

The physical touch shows love and most everyone responds to it. A tradition in our family was that whenever they did something that pleased me or that seemed to be in need of reward I would shake their hand and say, "I want to shake your hand for that!" They knew this was an act of love on my part and they responded in such a way one would have thought I had handed them a dollar bill.

I want to give you some very helpful and commanding scriptures God has given to us in discipling our children. If we obey his commandments and rear our children accordingly, we can relax and commit them completely into God's hands when they leave our nest and go out into the world. In turn this will give us complete freedom, knowing we were faithful to God in rearing them. Now he will be faithful in keeping them. They may wander away for a while, but God will see to it that they return to him. These scriptures you will want to memorize and hide away in your heart and mind. They are all found in Proverbs. "He that spareth his rod hateth his son: but he that loveth him chasteneth him betimes" (13:24). "Chasten thy son while there is hope, and let not thy soul spare for his crying" (19:18). "Train up a child in the way he should go: and when he is old, he will not depart from it" (22:6). "Foolishness is bound in the heart of a child; but the rod of correction shall drive it far from him" (22:15). "The rod and reproof give wisdom: but a child left to himself bringeth his mother to shame" (29:15). "Correct thy son, and he shall give thee rest; yea, he shall give delight unto thy soul" (29:17).

Never hesitate to ask the Lord for help with the problems you run into concerning your children. I share this experience with you by permission from Angie. She was three years old and I simply could not get her to use the potty-chair or toilet. I tried everything I knew. I stayed with her. I left her alone. I talked and talked, nothing worked. I was at the end of my rope. As I was praying one morning, I said, "Lord, will you please help me with this problem? Thank you." I neglected to tell you that Angie would come to me and ask me to put her diaper on (she wore training panties) when she had to go the potty. After my prayer, the next time Angie came to me asking me to put a diaper on her I took hold of her hand and these are the words that came out of my mouth, "Come on, Eleanor," (I had changed her identity; only God could have thought of that) "we are going upstairs to the potty." She went right along without fussing and used the potty and I used the name "Eleanor" several times after that and the problem was resolved.

If you love God, you will want to keep the commandments that he has given to us. If you are faithful in rearing your children in the admonition and knowledge of the Lord, your reward will be great.

My prayer for each mother reading this is found in Proverbs 31:28. "Her children arise up, and call her blessed; her husband also, and he praiseth her."

CHAPTER IX

"GOD'S TOP-DRAWER SECRETS"

"But seek ye first the kingdom of God, and his righteousness; and all these things shall be added unto you"

Matthew 6:33

How do you react when someone tells you he wants to share a secret with you? I get excited and thrilled to think he has chosen me for his confidante, don't you?

God has, in my opinion, five top-drawer secrets which, when received and practiced, will enable any Christian to live a victorious and joyful Christian life. The wonderful part about God's secrets is that he will share them with "whosoever will" ask for them to seek them. In Matthew 7:7 we read,

"Ask, and it shall be given; seek, and ye shall find; knock, and it shall be opened unto you." Perhaps you are a new Christian and you know nothing about God's secrets. I wish to open his top drawer, take out these secrets, and give them to you in the order in which I asked for them and received them.

The first secret I received was the power of confession. First John 1:9 says, "If we confess our sins, he is faithful and just to forgive us our sins, and to cleanse us from all unrighteousness." Not only does he forgive us our sins but he forgets them. The initial confession may be generalized as one admits he is a sinner, asks God to forgive his sins and come into his life that he might be with God forever. After one becomes a Christian, the Holy Spirit will speak to him or convict him when he sins; then one should be specific and confess each sin as he is convicted. A recording tape is an outstanding example of how, as individuals, we sin and it goes on record and stays there until we confess. Then God erases it, wipes it from our record, the same as tape on a recording machine. What is said is recorded on the tape but when the tape is wiped, the words, music, or whatever is gone forever. Tremendous spiritual power is generated by confessions. God truly hears our prayers when our lives are free from sin. "If I regard iniquity in my heart, the Lord will not hear me" (Psalm 66:18). Perhaps your prayers are going unanswered, no further than the ceiling. Examine yourself. Ask

God to tell you if you have unconfessed sins in your life and he will reveal them to you. "Search me, O God, and know my heart: try me, and know my thoughts: and see if there be any wicked way in me, and lead me in the way everlasting" (Psalm 139:23-24).

Oh look, the drawer is open again. What is this? God's second secret, "The Quiet Time." Perhaps new Christians haven't heard too much about this yet and you mature Christians may know all about it. You did have this as part of your daily life at one time, but you became so busy "helping God" you tucked this secret neatly back into the drawer. The "quiet time" is that time you set aside each day to spend with the Lord reading his word and talking to him. I prefer doing this as soon as possible after I arise in the morning. I like to *begin* the day with him, while others may choose another time during the day. One morning as I was quiet and listening for what God had to say to me, he said he would like to have the first fruit of my lips. He wanted me to say "good morning" to him before I spoke to anyone else. I find a tremendous blessing is mine by giving to God the first words of my lips each morning.

We should stay close to him all through the day, but God truly blesses us if we will faithfully set aside a "special time" for him consistently each day. Be systematic in your Bible reading. If you begin with the Gospel of John, begin with chapter one and read until you complete it, perhaps one or two chapters a day.

As your children observe you having your quiet time they, too, will imitate you, especially when they are small. They mirror our actions! When Angie, our fourteen-year-old, was about three, she came marching through the living room one evening with Bible in one hand and notebook and pencil in the other. Looking around at each of us, she said "Now I want you all to be quiet because I'm going to have my 'quiet time'". A three-year-old mirroring an example I was setting before her! I was not aware of her observance of me, but this little act on her part brought me to attention. I marveled at how our actions go into molding our children's characters. My talk with the Lord is a two-way conversation. I tell him what's on my heart and mind. Then I just sit and listen. If you listen he will speak to you. The more time you spend in listening, the more sensitive you will become to the still small voice of the Holy Spirit. If you truly want to be a disciple of Christ, you *must* keep a quiet time with him daily. If this secret is accepted and put into practice daily in your life, a definite change will take place. This second secret, the "quiet time" will teach you how to share Christ with others. It will radiate a special power in your life to be an effective and obedient Christian.

As I open the top drawer for the third time, out pops the third secret. "Put God into every detail of your life." Jesus is interested in every minute detail of your life—the tiny, frustrating, and irritating things like finding a parking place for your car downtown with so much traffic. Of course he is interested also in the big things. You have just been informed by your doctor your precious daughter has a malignant brain tumor. I can testify to the fact that if you put Christ into every detail, small or large, of your life, you can radiate peace and joy. I have had the experience of asking him to be in both of the situations mentioned above and many more I will share with you. He has never failed me and he won't fail you either because he says, "For there is no respect of persons with God" (Romans 2:11).

An elderly couple opened up God's top drawer and handed me this marvelous secret. I've always believed it was handed to me on a silver platter because when I made the decision to put God into every detail of my life, I felt that he opened up some special little window in heaven marked, "Betsy Patterson" and began to pour out the blessings upon me. I had been a Christian about a year when God placed me at a luncheon table with Mrs. Bowling. She began to tell story after story about how she and Mr. Bowling, being a retired man, helped the little children across the street at our corner. His face was always beaming. You could take one look at his face and see Christ shining forth. As I listened to Mrs. Bowling relate God-incidents—that's what I call them because they are not coincidences—I realized what a tremendous sense of humor God has, and why not? He is the ultimate in everything, even in humor.

One story she told depicts God's humor. She said they were planning a trip to California and were discussing the trip at the breakfast table. Mr. Bowling stated he thought they should get a lower berth and sleep together because she was always cold and from past experiences the train could be cold at night. She had a different idea. She thought they should take an upper and lower berth and sleep separately so they would be more comfortable. Mr. Bowling got up quickly from the table and said, "Well, dear, we haven't consulted the Lord on this matter," and with that went to their bedroom. Shortly he came forth with the Bible open and said, "It seems as though the Lord has settled the matter for us" and read to her from Ecclesiastes 4:11; "Again, if two lie together, then they have heat: but how can one be warm alone?" That settled it for me. I went home determined in my heart to begin to put God into everything. I have done so for twenty years. No doubt I've slipped now and again but when I do, I am the loser.

This may sound like a trifling thing to you but I know some women who are very embarrassed when they go to a luncheon meeting, or whatever, and see another woman come in with the same dress on that they are wearing. The next time ask the Lord what he would have you wear, and you will never see yourself. He knows what dress every woman will be wearing. When God reveals himself in the tiny things in my life it thrills me and enhances my love for him and my trust in him.

I'm writing this in the Madison Inn in Madison, Wisconsin. The Lord has given me two weeks here to complete his book. My husband is taking a special course here at the University and he brought me along. Each day I'm shut up with the Lord in Room 511. Since I'm in the room most of the day writing, I've been here the past two days when the college girls have cleaned the room. Monday just one girl came. I spoke to her and she grunted. It was obvious she didn't want to converse, so I said nothing more. Yesterday three girls came to clean and they didn't even open their mouths. This morning I said, "Please, Lord, send someone to clean who will talk." Two girls came in to clean, and one of them talked all the time she was in the room. A minute detail but God had answered my prayer.

God said in John 14:2, "I go to prepare a place for you." I always ask him to go ahead and get me a parking place, don't you? I want to share with you one precious incident. I was on my way to my obstetrician and halfway downtown I said, "Oh, Lord, I would especially appreciate a parking place right in front of the building because I'm on short time." Then I suddenly remembered I had changed purses and forgot to get the change purse out of the other purse so now I'm aware I'm without money. "Lord," I said, "you will not only have to get me a parking place but you will have to get me one with a meter that has enough time on it." As I turned the corner there it was right in front of the building. I said a quick, "Thank you, Lord," and got out of the car and looked at the meter. There was a whole hour on it. I was bubbling over. Only believe! That's our trouble most of the time, isn't it? Or we just don't bother to ask. He says in James 4:2 "Ye have not, because ye ask not."

Is he interested in the little things? Would you believe a cup and saucer? My husband and I were with some very dear friends of ours several days ago in their gift shop. We were admiring the lovely things and I happened to spot a shelf containing beautiful cups and saucers. I said, "I collect cups and saucers; my, you have such quaint ones." I had my eye on one done in what appeared to be tiny blue cross-stitches on white. I oh'ed and ah'ed over it and silently said, "Dear Lord please have Jack buy that for me." I no more breathed that prayer when my sweet husband said, "Honey, how would you like to have that little blue and white one?" I thanked the Lord and my husband for this outward show of love for me. Do we thank our husbands enough for all the little things they do for us? Nothing is too small or too big to bring to Jesus. I've had many people report to me that they began by taking a few little problems to him. Now they are taking everything to him and putting him into every detail of their lives. Praise the Lord!

Several years after I became a Christian, the Lord seemed to press a button on that top drawer and out it came. Right in front of me was the "spiritual law of acceptance." "What's that, Lord?" I asked, "What does that mean?" That still small voice whispered, "Accept what I permit to come your way whether you like it or not for my glory. Do things you do not wish to do to my glory and just see what happens."

Mother had come to live with us. We did many things alike but there were a few things in which we differed. One was the care of our wastebaskets. A minor thing, yes, but it bugged me. Mother insisted on putting paper bags in each basket to catch the trash. I had new baskets in various places. I enjoyed seeing the nice neat basket alone, not with a paper bag sticking out five inches. I mentioned it several times, but she always argued that it's so much easier to empty and keeps the basket cleaner. She would comply with my wishes for a while and then back the bags were again. I got tired of fussing, so I decided to take it to the Lord. That's when I learned about the spiritual law of acceptance. I said, "All right, Lord, I'll say nothing more. The paper bags in the wastebaskets are to your honor and glory." The Lord then changed my attitude. If you come and visit me anytime now, little paper bags peek out over the top of the baskets. Mother is still with us and has been for sixteen years. She is eighty-six, still is very sharp and continues to put paper bags in the wastebaskets.

I've found that if I do anything I dislike doing to the glory of Jesus or if I say, "I'm doing this just for you, Lord," this truly changes the whole picture and also changes my attitude or viewpoint.

One never knows how God is going to use his law of acceptance. I had a recent experience in which he changed the circumstances completely when and only when I accepted the situation. When we are praying for specific things we must be on our toes because sometimes God requires something of *us* before he answers our prayer. We had a situation in our home that had to be changed requiring a tremendous decision on my husband's part. The situation was definitely affecting each member of our family. We all prayed about it in our own way. The situation continued to get worse and worse, and my husband just couldn't seem to make the decision that was needed. At Christmas time, our daughter-in-law, Charlotte, Angie, and I were driving to one of the shopping centers. We were discussing this particular situation. Suddenly Charlotte turned to me and said, "Mom, I want to ask you a question and you will recognize it as something you said to me one time. Have you actually accepted the situation as it is?" Angie spoke up defending me and said, "I believe mom has." I pondered it all for a few seconds and I replied, "Charlotte, I have not accepted this situation. Oh, possibly I've thought I have, but in my heart I know I haven't unquestionably accepted this situation." I continued, "Possibly therein lies the answer." Later the Holy Spirit also brought to my mind that he had tried to give me a hint of this a month before when our other daughter-in-law Becky had given us a gift of an embroidered plaque which read: "God grant me the serenity to accept the things I cannot change, courage to change those things I can, and wisdom to know the difference." When she gave it to us, I simply didn't get the message.

As I stood at my sink I mulled over and over all that had been said. Several weeks later I arose quite early one morning to be alone with the Lord to talk this thing over with him. I confessed first the resentment and antagonism I had harbored toward this situation. After confessing, I blurted out, "Lord, with the grace you have already extended to me and that grace I know you will continue to give I accept this situation." Oh, what comfort I experienced. Would you believe that within a week my husband made that very difficult decision that removed the entire situation from our home. We all have complete peace about every detail. Here again God wants to do for us if we will but permit him to do so. God does have his spiritual laws, and the spiritual law of acceptance is one of them. May I add, be open and willing to learn from your daughters-in-law. They may impart priceless advice to you that you wouldn't be able to find elsewhere. At the wedding of each of our sons I felt God gave us a daughter and I consider each one a gift from him with his love.

The top drawer was opened once again to me through two verses of Scripture. One in 1 Thessalonians 5:18: "In every thing give thanks, for this is the will of God in Christ Jesus concerning you." The other in Philippians 4:6 "In every thing by prayer and supplication with thanksgiving let your requests be made known unto God." That was a memorable time. I determined I would thank God in everything—the good and the bad. It wasn't long until he tested me. Mother and I were in the kitchen preparing a meal. I opened the refrigerator. When I took hold of the handle on the top of a glass jug of milk, the entire square bottom fell off. One gallon of milk was distributed over the Patterson's kitchen floor. I was startled for a minute; then I started laughing and said, "Praise the Lord, thank you, Lord." When I glanced at mother she looked horrified. "What in the world are you thanking him for? Milk all over this floor?" "Mother, haven't you ever heard there's nothing better for linoleum than giving it a good milk bath?" I had no idea that when I made the decision to thank the Lord in all things, good or bad, that he would test my decision in this way. With a thanksgiving attitude nothing is difficult to do. I quickly had the milk cleaned up and the floor looked beautiful! I continued a while in this but about a year ago I read an outstanding book that made me realize I had put this secret back into God's top drawer.

I have never felt the presence of the Holy Spirit when reading a book like I did while I was reading this one about giving thanks in all things, good and bad. After completing the book I opened that top drawer again and retrieved this secret. I am again practicing it in my daily life as never before. It truly is a powerful secret at your disposal anytime. I could cite incident after incident of how God handles situations when we praise him for them. It's easy to thank him for the good; more difficult to thank him for the bad.

Mil Gerig, my dear friend, and I had just regained our composure after escaping a near serious accident. We had thanked God for this and were on our way once again heading toward Bloomington, Illinois, where I was to speak to the Christian Women's Club. We were pressed for time, being expected by noon. All was going well when we heard a terrible noise. Mil said, "Now what?" With that she was out of the car to see. She came back shaking her head and lamenting, "We have a flat tire." I said, "Let's pray. Thank you, Lord, for this flat tire. We don't know why you let this happen, but would you please send someone to help us?" We just raised our heads in time to see a truck slowing down on the opposite side of the road. The man quickly came back to us and said, "Well, it looks like you ladies need help." He changed the tire in a very short time and refused one penny for his work. Again we thanked our Father and arrived at the meeting on schedule.

I want to share another incident that took place on that trip proving there is tremendous power in thanking God for the bad. I had an engagement to speak at one o'clock in a university town in Illinois. I arrived about 12:45. Three of us retired to a little chapel room for prayer on a floor above the room where the meeting was to be held. We shut the door and each prayed in turn. It was just a few minutes before one o'clock and we were all to be on the platform at one. The chairman went to the door and turned the knob. Nothing happened. She turned it again and again, but nothing happened. The door would not open. She looked at us and said, "Ladies, we are locked in." I said, "Praise the Lord, now we can see him perform a miracle."

I walked over to the door and stooped down to see what kind of lock it had on it and saw not only one bar across but two. I turned to the women and said, "Ladies, there are two bars across that door. We are doubly locked in. Praise the Lord, let's pray." The chairman said, "You pray." I prayed something like this, "Lord, thank you for locking us in. You know we are supposed to be on the platform by one o'clock and the only reason we want to be there is to glorify you. Now we need a miracle to get us out of here. Thank you, in Jesus' name, Amen." I took hold of the doorknob and turned it toward my left side and the door opened and we walked out. One of the ladies said, "Praise the Lord." Someone else said, "Hallelujah." We walked into the meeting. No one was the wiser, but I had a spanking brand-new miracle to share with all of them. Frances Hunter would now say, "God is fabulous!" I couldn't agree more, Frances.

CHAPTER X

"THIS AND THAT—A LITTLE OF BOTH"

> *"Now faith is the substance of things hoped for, the evidence of things not seen"*
> —Hebrews 11:1

> *"Faith cometh by hearing, and hearing by the word of God"*
> —Romans 10:17

I have found in living the Christian style of life that faith is a coveted possession. Everyone seems to want it. Invariably after I have spoken to a group of people someone will come up to me and say, "I wish I had your kind of faith," or, "Yes, I know things like you have been speaking about come if you have faith but I guess I just don't have it." Some have come right to the point and asked, "How do you get faith?" The answer to this is found in the verse above, Hebrews 11:1. In my experience I have found that *anything* I have that is worthwhile I have paid a price for. Faith is no different. It comes into our lives as we consistently, day after day, read the Bible. There is no mystery to it. The more you read the inspired Word of God, faith increases in your life. If at this moment you are trying to whip up enough faith in your own strength to trust God for a particular thing, that's the wrong approach. You must get into the Bible and begin to read. Another way I've found that faith can be increased is to share it with someone else. Possibly someone is saying, "What does she mean by that?" If you have read a verse or verses in the Bible that have meant something special to you, ask God to send someone your way with whom you can share it. Faith in God or trusting God in all things is the most valuable asset I have. The more you read the Bible, the more you trust him, the more he reveals himself to you. Then it comes naturally; you desire to trust him even more. It's an unending cycle.

I want to share with you some experiences that have been enjoyed by myself and others through trusting God. This is what Christianity is all about —a trust in the Lord, whether it be for a lost soul or for your next meal. God always honors faith or trust.

After speaking at a mother-daughter banquet one evening, several people were talking with me when I noticed a little girl about seven or eight standing at the side waiting to say something to me. I excused myself from the women, went over to the little girl, and asked her if I could help her. She asked me if I would pray for her daddy. She said he wasn't a Christian and he made it very difficult for the rest of the family, especially her mother. We went aside from the crowd and I asked her if she knew the verse in Matthew 18:19, "That if two of you shall agree on earth as touching any thing that they shall ask, it shall be done for them of my Father which is in heaven." She assured me she knew the verse. We agreed that we both would begin praying and thanking God for her daddy's salvation. I took the request to my Bible study groups and they joined us in prayer. Several months later she called me and said nothing had happened and would I continue to pray. I said I would and encouraged her to continue to pray and to believe that God was working. I had another call from her at Christmastime saying that things were really bad at her house, that her daddy didn't want them to go to church and that he had struck her mother. (The one thing I couldn't help thinking about was that I had never talked with her mother; all the conversations had been with this little girl.)

Several more months passed. One morning the phone rang at 8:15. It was my little friend. She was very excited. She told me her daddy had gone forward and accepted Christ as Lord and Savior in a revival meeting at their church the night before. Needless to say I, too, was thrilled and excited. Something happened just yesterday in which I believe God gave me his confirmation that I was supposed to share this story with you. I was at a refresher retreat here in Fort Wayne. After the

meeting a young mother introduced herself as my
little friend's mother. We had a wonderful visit and
she seemed very happy I was including their story
in my book.

People love to hear stories in which one tells
about their walk in faith. As Christian parents we
should encourage our children to trust the Lord in
all things as they are growing and maturing physically and spiritually. This God-incident is about
David, our older son. It took place when he was in
grade school. It was the day before Halloween and
the children were to come to school costumed and
then march from room to room. That year David
needed a new costume. That morning I went to
town and bought one I thought he would like.
When the children came home for lunch, I showed
him the costume and he didn't like it. The other
children were getting into their costumes but he
was still complaining and arguing with me that he
didn't want to wear his. He was very disappointed
and flared up in anger. He flatly stated he didn't
like it, and he wasn't going to wear it. I tried to
reason with him to no avail. At the peak of our ar-
gument his daddy walked in. When he learned
what the problem was he said, "All right, since you
feel this way about it, David, you can go to school
without a costume." He meant every word he said
and David and I knew he meant it. David began
to cry and was brokenhearted about the whole af-
fair but he knew he would have to obey his dad.

After issuing this ultimatum my husband left the room.

I sat down with our David and said to him, "Let's pray about this, honey. Why don't you ask God to forgive you for becoming angry and then ask him if he will take care of you in his way this afternoon?" He stopped crying and prayed as I suggested. He washed his face and left me with peace, trusting the Lord for the afternoon. Every time he came to my mind I thanked God for what he was doing for David. This incident would not be complete by my telling you we trusted the Lord and received peace but I want to go on and tell you how God honored and blessed David for trusting him. When David returned from school that afternoon, he was bursting with his news. When he arrived at the school, the principal saw he was without a costume. He called him into his office and asked him why. David told him the whole story about what had happened at home. Without further ado the principal proceeded to "fix him up" a costume. It was so original that David was more pleased than he could ever have been with a "store bought" costume. David also realized that the promise in 1 John 1:9 is true and what God says he means, "If we confess our sins, he is faithful and just to forgive us our sins, and to cleanse us from all unrighteousness." He knew God had forgiven him and loved him for saying he was sorry. God truly honors our faith and trust in him and blesses us for it.

We should constantly be on our toes as to God's leading and then obey and trust his leading. Several years ago I was conducting a Bible study once a month in our circle meeting in the church I was then attending. At the beginning of the study I asked the Lord to allow one woman to come to know him personally through the study. At our first meeting I mentioned the Bible study course I led in my home each week. After the meeting a young woman came up to me and asked me if she could join my home Bible study group. Of course the answer was yes. I knew immediately that this was the person the Lord had given me to concentrate upon. She did join my group and in a very few weeks she gave her life to the Lord. Soon she led her husband to the Lord, and then the children followed one by one. God's word in Proverbs 11:30, says, "He that winneth souls is wise."

Do you pray for your enemies? Jesus says in Matthew 5:44 that we should pray for our enemies. Whenever I come in contact with a person who doesn't seem to warm up to me or seems to be on the defensive, I begin to pray for that person. I pray for his welfare and for his salvation if he does not appear to know the Lord. A woman and I were asked to decorate a tea table. We were given the materials with which to do this and were instructed to come early the day of the tea to perform this task. I arrived at the appointed time and waited and waited, but when the other woman didn't come I finally began "doing" the table. I had it completed and thought it had that "just right" look. Some other ladies standing nearby agreed. About that time the woman who was to help me arrived on the scene. She began to change things around. I felt myself becoming a little unhappy with her until the Holy Spirit reminded me of the words of Jesus in Matthew 5:46, "For if ye love them which love you, what reward have ye? do not even the publicans the same?" I kept my mouth shut and decided to pray for her instead. I did pray for her.

At our next meeting she came up to me and asked if I had any little devotional books I might let her read. I gave her several that I thought might give her an insight into a personal relationship with the Lord. Several days later she called me and said she had read the pamphlets but she didn't feel any different and nothing had changed for her. I asked her to come and talk with me. She did and I talked to her about the things of the Lord. As she left I gave her Eugenia Price's book, *The Burden is Light.* About a week later my doorbell rang. When I opened the door, there stood my dear friend. She was smiling and her face shone with a great light. I knew what had happened just by looking at her. I could see Christ had taken hold of her. She could wait no longer. She said, "Oh, I have something wonderful to tell you." Eagerly I said, "Come in and tell me all about it."

This was the story she told me: One night she couldn't sleep and so she got up and decided to read the book I had given her. It was about two o'clock on a very hot night, so she had all the windows and doors open. She sat down on her sofa, cigarette in one hand, the book in the other. She said she came to the part in the book where Genie Price told her story of how she gave up smoking. My friend said right then and there she thought, "That's what Jesus wants *me* to do." She said, "All right, Lord, if that's what you want of me, I'm willing to give it up." She said she laid down her cigarette. At that moment a mighty wind rushed in through the window, engulfed her, and rushed out the door. She said it lasted only a moment, but she knew just at that time the Holy Spirit had entered her soul and she felt clean. She knew she belonged to the Lord Jesus Christ. How I praised God for another soul that had been brought into his kingdom.

She had many problems. One was that her husband was an alcoholic. She began to study God's Word and pray. She grew spiritually by leaps and bounds. Before the year was up they moved to California. I received several letters from her telling about the changes that had come into her life. Her husband stopped drinking and began attending church with her. The last I heard she had joined a Bible study group and was witnessing to others about the greatness of our Christ.

You've had a little of "this" now I'll give you a little of "that." I've mentioned many times in this book about trusting God for small details. I remember the day I trusted him for tomatoes. I had so much to do that day preparing for guests for dinner that night that I knew I didn't have time to go to the grocery and get the tomatoes I needed for the dinner salad. I prayed, "Lord, I could serve the salad without tomatoes but it is so much better with them; if somehow you could supply them I would be ever so grateful." Around five-thirty that afternoon Angie came into the house and said, "Mother, here's a sack for you from Grandma Weber (Grandma Weber lives next door to us). I looked into the sack and there were big, luscious, red tomatoes. God is so good.

If we encourage faith in our children, we will see the fruit of our efforts. Angie came back to our room one Sunday afternoon all excited. She said, "Mother, Mort (her brother) just told me that he and Becky (his girl friend at that time) put my name in a box for a drawing on a pony. He said they could put in as many slips as they wanted to, so they put in five with my name on it." She ran out of the room and then suddenly she was back. "Mother," she said, "do you know what I just did?" "No," I replied, "What did you do?" "I asked God to let me win one of those ponies." I was flabbergasted. Where would we put a pony. I quickly said, "Angie, did you say, Thy will be done?" "Oh, yes, mother. I said, Thy will be done."

Our family was leaving the house that afternoon to attend a fiftieth-wedding anniversary celebration. Angie casually said to grandma, "Grandma, please call me when they call and tell you I've won the pony." We went on to the party. While I was in conversation with several people, I heard a conversation going on at my right side between Mort and Angie. "Now, Angie," Mort said, "I saw how many names were in that box and you just don't have a chance, so forget it." "But, Mort, I asked God to give me one of those ponies and I know he will." Mort gave up and that ended their conversation. About an hour later I was called to the phone; it was grandma. "Betsy, you just can't imagine what's happened?" "No, mother, I can't. What has happened?" Angie *won* that pony! And in addition to that she won the saddle and bridle." "Praise the Lord," I said, "Isn't that great?" "But Betsy, wait a minute, I have something else to tell you. The man who called said when they drew out the first name it was Angie's and then when they drew out the second name it was also Angie's." Now I said, "Hallelujah!" I was really bubbling with this bit of news because no one now could call that a coincidence. God had answered a child's prayer. If we could all trust him like a little child, more prayers would be answered.

If anyone is reading this who is frightened to ride in an airplane, perhaps my experience with this fear might be helpful. My brother's wife was to have surgery. My mother thought it would be very helpful to my brother and his family if I would go out to their home in Texas for the time my sister-in-law was in the hospital. Mother and my husband decided I should fly and, before I could think about it, my husband had my ticket and everything set for me to fly. It was to be my first plane ride and I did feel quite edgy about it. At the last minute I picked up a little devotional book I had been using in my quiet time and stuck it in my purse. After we had taken off, I began to feel such a sense of fear I became panicky. Then I thought of the little book tucked away in my purse. I got it out and turned to the devotional for that particular date. What should meet my eyes but the title, "Why Travel the Hard Way?" I just stopped and thought about that for a few minutes. It seemed as if the Lord was saying, "Just think a moment, I've given you the blessing of this lovely plane ride and you are fretting and being fearful. Can't you trust me?" I felt so ashamed. I thanked him for the trip and asked him to forgive me. A deep sense of peace came to me and I had a wonderful trip to Texas. He is always with us. The Bible says, "He will never leave us nor forsake us."

I've related several experiences illustrating how God honors and blesses our faith in him. We pray, but do we believe he hears and will answer? "Now faith is the substance of things hoped for, the evidence of things not seen" (Hebrews 11:1).

CHAPTER XI

"LOVE IN BLOOM"

"Write this for a memorial in a book"

—Exodus 17:14.

This morning as I pen these words I'm shut up with God in Room 511 in the Madison Inn in Madison, Wisconsin. God has set aside these two weeks for me to complete "his book" I began so long ago. As I begin the second week I sense it has been a difficult task, but God always balances the scale with blessings. It has been good to be here with my husband who is studying at the University. I'm thankful for the rest (in between the periods of writing) it has afforded, and most of all, I'm indeed grateful for the quiet times I've had with Jesus. To give out we must always be taking in.

This chapter will be a heart-to-heart talk from me to you. Up to now you may have had a few chuckles. Now you may shed a few tears, but laughter and tears seem to be twins as we live the Christian style of life.

I do not wish to impress you that living the Christian life is a bed of roses, because it isn't. Even though life is filled with trials, problems, and sorrows, when you walk with *Jesus* daily through these, it is completely different. At first the trial may appear as a thorn but if you will see the rose, Jesus, by your side sharing it with you, he can turn that trial into joy. I felt a real surge of joy bubble up within me the morning I read that beautiful verse: Psalm 56:8. To think he puts each of my tears, and yours too, into a bottle and is saving them to be poured out unto him as sweet smelling odors. The eighth verse says, "Thou tellest my wanderings: put thou my tears into thy bottle: are they not in thy book?" Just stop a moment and think. He is implying that he also is recording in a book each time you shed a tear. Never be ashamed of tears. Jesus wept over the death of Lazarus.

I have had my trials during these past twenty years, but never once did God make me walk alone. He always had his hand extended toward me if I but took it. The promise that God has given to us when he said that his grace is sufficient for your every need was beautifully fulfilled in our family in 1966. I promised the Lord I would honor and glorify him in telling our Becky's story. The Lord also told me, through the verse he gave to me one morning, that he wanted me to write her story in a book as a memorial to her. I had asked to whom should I dedicate his book and this verse came as the answer. "Write this for a memorial in a book" (Exodus 17:14). I praise him for his continual guidance.

Becky's story is a "love story" from the beginning to the end. I once heard this definition of love: "It's a tickling sensation around the heart that you can't scratch." That's a trite or trivial definition of love. If we want to have a vivid and true explanation of what true love is, all we need to do is turn to the thirteenth chapter of First Corinthians where Paul tells us what constitutes real love, "love in bloom." Perhaps some teen-agers are reading this. You believe you are in love. Why do you think you are? If you are old enough to date, you believe you are in love because you just *love* being with him or her. When you see him or her, you feel little chills go all over you. You would be content just to sit in his or her presence even if you didn't say a word to each other. Oh, you believe you are *so* in love. It just thrills you to think of the word *love*.

As I said before, Becky's story is a story about love, not love for the opposite sex but about her love for Jesus. A love so in bloom that it has been described by a songwriter as a "love that will not let you go." God talks about his love for us in John 3:16. This is the ultimate in love. God's First Commandment to Christians is to love him with all our heart, soul, and mind. This is "love in bloom," and this Becky did! She allowed Jesus to come into her heart at a very tender age. It all happened in a child evangelism class held in our grade school after school was dismissed, one afternoon a week. I praise God for women who are permitting him to use them to point "the way" to these precious children. From the moment Becky confessed her sins and accepted Jesus into her heart and life she lived for him and lived to please him.

God gave Becky a wonderful gift—the ability to become a musician. She began to take lessons on the oboe when she was in the third grade. We lived in Waukegan, Illinois at the time. All the grade schools had children representing their school in two different bands—the Junior Band and the Concert Band. Becky was proficient enough to go directly into the Concert Band. This outstanding band for many years was well-known throughout the United States. While listening to the music rendered by these young people, ages ranging nine through twelve, one could believe he was listening to senior high school or university students. At the age of eleven, while playing in a concert one night, Becky was discovered by Dr. Joseph Maddy, founder of the Interlochen Music Camp, Interlochen, Michigan. At this particular concert he was the guest conductor. He offered Becky a scholarship to the music camp for that summer. His wife, a very dear friend of ours, told us months later that her husband came home after that concert and said he had lost his heart to another woman; then continued to tell her about Becky.

Becky accepted the scholarship and attended the music camp that summer. She loved every minute of the eight weeks spent there. She gained so much from this experience that we decided she should again attend the camp the following summer. Little did we realize the importance of this decision. It was during camp that summer that Dr. Maddy and the music department heads decided that Becky should receive a thousand-dollar scholarship for each of the next four years at the new Interlochen Arts Academy High School which would entitle her to a charter membership.

While we were attending the Convocation exercises at the end of the camp period Dr. Maddy and others talked with my husband and me about Becky's musical ability, pleading with us to permit her to skip the eighth grade and enter the academy as a freshman. When they saw we were reluctant because of her tender age, they assured us she was capable. They backed this up by telling us the director of admissions at the University of Michigan had interviewed Becky and had found she was mature in every way to take this step.

My husband and I asked if they would give us a little time to think this over. We wanted to talk to Becky that we might know her feelings about all this. We promised we would give them a yes or no answer before we took her home. They agreed to this. My husband and I found Becky completely ecstatic about the whole idea. "May I, oh, please may I?" she kept repeating over and over again. My husband and I finally agreed we were willing to permit her to leave home and attend high school there, but the one thousand dollars a year was just one-third of the yearly cost. Our son

David was just beginning his first year in college. We knew that cost would be great and we simply could not swing this whole thing. While the three of us were discussing how we could ever manipulate the finances involved, my husband told us he had to get away alone to think about this. Becky and I sat down on the steps of her cabin in the woods where she had spent the summer.

After we had talked together for what seemed to us a long time, we looked up to see her daddy winding his way back to us through the trees. We were so eager for his answer we ran to meet him. His face was beaming with a smile and we really knew the answer before asking. He quickly said, "Well, Becky, I told Dr. Maddy you can come up here to high school." She gave a little squeal. He then looked at me and said, "Betts, (his pet name for me) I'm going to do like you are always saying: step out on faith and trust God. All right, we'll trust God for the money we are going to need." Needless to say we were three happy people. Several weeks later, back in Fort Wayne, God proved to me once again, beyond a shadow of a doubt that he honors and blesses those who trust him. My husband was not a Christian at this time. Through a set of very personal circumstances God not only provided the amount of money needed for Becky's schooling that year but he also provided for the entire amount needed for David's college. As we allowed Becky to leave us and attend high school many miles from home I could see

God's grace in action. Humanly, it should have been very difficult for us but God's grace was sufficient for this need. Happiness was hers for being able to see a dream come true. Since we knew *loving* means also freedom, we let her go to develop her musical ability. As I now look back, God was using this period of time to wean us from one another.

Becky so loved the Lord during her four years at Interlochen she shared him with many people telling what he meant in her life. Jan, Becky's closest friend at Interlochen, once told me: "I saw that Becky had something I wanted and I asked her one day what it was. She told me all about Christ, what he had done in her life, for her and through her. Consequently, I, too, accepted him!" Jan is a lovely, young Christian woman today, living her life for him. Becky had a great influence on many people at Interlochen, we have been told, by teachers and counselors there.

In July of 1965, between her junior and senior years, she became ill and it was learned through surgery that she had a rare, malignant brain tumor. I would like to pause here to encourage those of you who are praying for a loved one to accept Christ to keep on praying. We never know when God is going to answer or what he will use to answer our prayer. I had been praying for my husband to accept Christ for fifteen years. I had tried to live the Christian life before him daily. During those fifteen years each of our children had accepted Christ and we were all praying for daddy. Many of my friends were also praying for him. He told me once, "I was a hard nut to crack." No, I thought, it wasn't that, it was God's timing; his timing is not always our timing. We are impatient but I have learned that the "Lord's hand is not shortened, that it cannot save" (Isaiah 59:1).

The surgeon came to the waiting lounge after Becky's first surgery. I was waiting there with our faithful pastor, Mr. Mitchell, and friends. The doctor explained to me that the tumor they had removed from Becky's brain was malignant. We later learned it was a very rare type of malignancy. I felt God's peace totally surround me. The children and I stood calm and peaceful in the eye of this storm. My husband happened to be in the doctor's lounge when the surgeon gave him the news. Jack was completely shattered. He didn't know The One who would have taken his hand and led him through this calmly. It happened that our David was working as an orderly at another hospital. A kind friend called him and told him about Becky. He was on the scene immediately. Our younger son, Mort, also came to the hospital right away. Angie, seven years old at the time, was home with grandma. David went to the recovery room where Becky had been taken and asked if he could care for her while she was there. The nurses were just great and said he could.

The doctor told me I might go into the recovery room. What joy I felt when I saw David caring for

Becky! I couldn't help but think of God's goodness again leading David to become an orderly if only for this task. Here again we see God in a detail, he's always there if we see him. While I was standing there in the recovery room the door opened and there was my precious Jack, tears streaming down his face. He came over to me, put his arms around me and said, "Betts, I need help." All the words that I had said in the past to him quickly raced through my mind, but at that moment no words came. A dead silence and then he said, "I have an appointment with our minister at seven-thirty this evening at the church." My heart was praising God as I let him go.

Later on in the evening Becky was taken from the recovery room to her own room. David, Mort, and I were in the room when Jack returned. As he walked through the door I knew he had met Jesus. His face showed utter peace and trust. I knew he had met the *only* person that gives not only life eternal with him but also can take us through any circumstance that occurs in our lives. I was very quiet, thinking he was going to tell us all about what had happened to him, but Jack is not like I am. He is quiet and reserved and I had to wait patiently until he was ready to tell us.

When I heard his story the next day I truly believe I've never before or since experienced such mixed emotions. Sheer joy filled my soul as he related his experience to our Becky at her bedside. I was sitting on the sidelines listening and then, too, a real sadness to realize what it had taken to bring him to Christ. The one thing he said to Becky that will never leave my mind, which he has probably forgotten, was this: "Becky, now I'm inside the family; I'm no longer on the outside looking in." At different times while she was in the hospital, he brought her Bible verses that brought heavenly sunshine into her soul. When she became ill and learned it possibly was something in her brain, she said to me, "Mother, I would be willing to die and go to be with the Lord if it would bring daddy to Christ Jesus." A sixteen-year-old saying that. Spiritual maturity? Yes! Also that great love the Bible speaks of as laying ourselves down to die for a friend, only in this case her daddy.

Once again I say don't give up praying and trusting God for that loved one you are praying for because there is *no* hopeless case with God—that alcoholic, that young man or girl on dope. No, nothing is impossible with God.

In that year and a half, Becky went through three major operations. She snapped back to normal so rapidly after each surgery that she never really seemed to be ill. She never complained, always had a smile, and was constantly endeavoring to help someone else.

One evening on my way to the hospital to visit with Becky, I knew I was later than I intended to be and began lamenting the fact to her as I entered her room. She said, "Oh, mother it turned out just the way God wanted it, as one of my friends came to visit me and she just left." She continued to tell me how her friend questioned her as to how she could take all of this, how she could be so joyful and happy. "Mom," she said, "it was such a wonderful opportunity to tell her about my friend Jesus and that in everything I've been through he has never left me. *He* is the one who gives me the joy and strength for each day."

My husband's partner died that year with a malignancy. Several times he mentioned to us what a help Becky had been to him. While he was at Mayo's his room happened to be just down the hall from Billy Graham's. Dr. Graham visited him and gave him one of his books. Hearing this, I was led by the Holy Spirit to write to Dr. Graham telling him of Becky's courage and her deep and abiding faith in God. Grady Wilson answered as Billy Graham dictated the reply, stating he had read my letter over and over again to some of the physicians and staff who visited him and he assured us that the letter was a profound witness among many. Billy Graham proved to us, by this gesture of love, that he identifies with the little people as well as the great.

God's loving grace was demonstrated through Becky one afternoon just after she had learned she was to have the second surgery. She was sitting in the middle of our bed, cross-legged, talking to her dad and me. She was explaining to us her heartfelt reaction to facing this number two surgery. Her dad had just said, "Becky, I want you to know we have just begun to fight." She didn't want us to be upset about this news. She said to him it was just like at school. When she had learned and could play well one piece of music, then she was given another to tackle and such was her life. God was taking her on to the new lesson he had for her to learn. Jack and I and the rest of our family, as well as our friends, can vouch that Becky learned each lesson well. God used Becky's sense of humor to get her over many rough spots. We know God is the ultimate in all things, even in humor. I saw her sense of humor come forth even in tragic moments. For each of her two surgeries her head had to be shaved. I recall her laughing at her bald head as she was combing her wig. A sixteen-year-old! Listening to her giggles, I was amazed at her spiritual maturity but still I shouldn't have been, because I knew God was honoring my faithfulness in having daily devotions with our children during those formative years. Wigs had just come into vogue, the timing again was right. How grateful to God I was for this blessing!

God is always there if we look up and see him. It was a week before Christmas when our surgeon told us Becky had three months to live. He felt we should tell her as she had a right to know. After all it was her life! He believed *we* were the ones to tell her. We agreed. At home standing at my kitchen window, it all hit me like a thunder bolt. This just *can't* be happening to us, I thought, but then the next thought came, No, we aren't immune.

Tragedy hits all people everywhere. We have to tell her she has only three months to live. Oh, God, no, we simply can't tell her this. There was complete silence in my kitchen. I was alone with God! Suddenly I remembered something I had read in one of Genie Price's books. She had said she was going through a trial. She just told God she was going to claim and believe his promise that his grace was sufficient for her every need. Genie went on to say that since she was a woman of action, she just lifted her arms into the air and said, "God, I need your grace just now." She was ready to receive it and God gave it to her. He flooded her soul, mind, and body with perfect peace. I repeated Genie's performance and I, too, received the peace and grace that passeth all understanding. It seemed to flow from me into my husband, then into Becky, as we told her. After we finished telling her, our pastor, bless him, arrived at the precise moment we needed prayer. Following the prayer Becky got up from the sofa, threw her little shoulders back and said, "Well, we aren't going to let this spoil our Christmas. We are going to celebrate Christ's birthday this year like we have never celebrated it before." We did just that and have done likewise each Christmas since that time.

As I shopped for gifts for Becky that year I knew these would be the last gifts I would ever buy for her. God led me to every piece of clothing I purchased. All the gifts seemed to be more pleasing and appreciated by her than ever before.

Mort's girl friend, Becky, had a coat she had bought several months before Christmas that our Becky truly admired. Mort and Becky set out to find another coat exactly like hers. They searched the town from one end to the other and finally found the coat. Oh, how thrilled and excited our Becky was when she opened that package! I can still see the glow on her face as she modeled it for us.

On Christmas morning I was in the kitchen preparing food for our dinner. Becky came into the kitchen and said, "Mom, will you check this card for me. I want your approval." The card was one she was going to enclose with a gift to her doctor who had become a real friend to her as well as her surgeon. They had a mutual love and appreciation for music. She had chosen some records she believed he would enjoy as her gift to him. Through tears I could not see what the card was like. All I could see was the Scripture verse she had written at the bottom: Philippians 4:11 and 12, "For I have learned, in whatsoever state I am, therewith to be content. I know both how to be abased, and I know how to abound." God's grace?? How could I ever question it!

Becky did complete her senior year. She graduated with honors as a charter member of the academy. That was her greatest desire and God fulfilled it. She said, "God truly loves me to have allowed me to graduate from high school." During that year God demonstrated his love toward all of us by giving her strength to play a solo with the Fort Wayne Philharmonic orchestra.

During the summer months Becky worked eight weeks for her daddy, all the while taking large doses of medication including cortisone. Many changes took place in her physical makeup but she never complained. Jack and I are so grateful for those months we had with her because we became very close. We saw more of her inner beauty brought about by Christ indwelling her. She was sheer joy to be around and Jack, the family, and I learned much from her. I believe that whole year was God's miracle year of love in Becky's life.

We did everything humanly possible and I couldn't estimate the prayers that went up to the throne of grace for her. The last week in September Becky started going downhill. We kept her home as long as possible. Our heavenly Father led us to have a beautiful communion service in the bedroom the last day she was home. Our family, with our pastor, Reverend Mitchell, participated in this meaningful experience. That night she began having excruciating pain necessitating hypos. She reminded me how grateful she was that, being a nurse, I could administer these to her.

Early Saturday morning she told us that she felt we should take her to the hospital because of Angela, her eight-year-old sister. Becky realized how hard it was for Angela to see her in pain. Before we took her to the hospital Saturday noon, she said lovingly to me, "Mom, don't you become alarmed or sad if I become unconscious because *I'll be back*" and I know she will be. When Christ returns Becky will be with him.

Her pain was controlled with hypos. Late Saturday night she slipped into a coma, breathing normally all the while. This continued only until Monday evening when she slipped through the door into the arms of the heavenly angels and was lifted higher and higher into Paradise with Jesus. Paul said to the Christians at Corinth in 2 Corinthians 5:8, "We are confident, I say, and willing rather to be absent from the body, and to be present with the Lord." How grateful we are that we have the wonderful assurance that Becky is with our Lord, perfect in every way.

Becky and I sang a little chorus when the pain in her head became unbearable. It was, "Praise Be to the Lord, Hallelujah." Over and over again we sang those words in the car, at home, and at the hospital. They always brought comfort and peace to her. Believe me there is power in praising God in the hard places. After Becky breathed her last breath I found my way quietly to the foot of her bed and sang the chorus for the last time, alone, but I'm sure her voice was joining mine as she walked into the arms of Jesus. No, I truly could not have done this in my own strength but I did it in the power of the Holy Spirit of God. Even in death he can give power to praise him if we are willing.

The verse she chose that year for her very own was Philippians 1:21, "For to me to live is Christ, and to die is gain." Our minister, without knowing this, chose this verse to use in the devotional he gave at her funeral. This is an example of how God works all things together for good to those who love him. He loves us so much he wants to take care of the tiniest details in our lives if we will but let him.

Becky's funeral was beautiful, held in our church, with her Interlochen friends as pallbearers. Many hearts were touched and lives changed through Reverend Mitchell's marvelous message. He said Becky's courage and faith during her illness inspired him to dedicate the following poem to her memory:

> For me to live is Jesus Christ
> To testify and teach
> And take the gospel of my Lord
> To those that I can reach.
> Oh yes, I'll serve Him day by day
> And go where He may lead.
> And I will live this life of mine
> To help some soul in need.

Many people lived through this year with us. Many have told us they truly searched God's word, spent more time in prayer than ever before, and were brought closer to God. New prayer warriors came into being who had neglected their prayer lives. Others marveled that all of us could live joyfully with death as a constant companion, but the Twenty-Third Psalm says, "Yea, though I walk through the valley of the shadow of death, I will fear no evil: for Thou art with me."

You might ask what of our prayers and those of beloved Christians who cried out for God to heal our daughter. We discovered that God always heals, but sometimes the results are greater, the fruits more abundant, if he waits until we're in heaven with him.

My mother heart will not allow me to say, "No, she did not," to so frequent a question, Did she suffer? Of course she suffered, physically and mentally. It was part of her ministry. But I believe for every pain and hurt she won a jewel in her crown. God has told us in his Word that there are those who will suffer according to his will, but he will never fail them for he is a faithful Creator. I think we, too, experienced and can understand what Catherine Marshall meant when she said concerning her husband's death, "It was as if God left the door ajar when our loved one entered into his presence and some of the joy and glory filtered out into our very beings."

Only God knows the complete results from Becky's life. She must have been crowned at her coronation with, "Well done, thou good and faithful servant," by Jesus' own lips. He worked through her and taught all of us deeper things of God: abiding faith, patience, and a realization that he truly carried our sorrows and bore our grief on the way to the cross. So we feel *no grief*, and this is a miracle above all miracles!

God does love you and me! He gives us joy when we have sorrow. He can give us perfect peace that can't be understood when we have insurmountable problems. We read in the Bible that "perfect love casteth out fear." Becky did not fear death. She knew she had eternal life. She knew Jesus had her hand in his. As she walked through the door known to us as physical death five days before her seventeenth birthday, we were grateful to our heavenly Father that he allowed her to be with us seven months longer than we had expected.

"Lord, you commanded me to write this book as a memorial to Becky. I pray that this chapter telling her story has glorified and honored you. I have done as you commanded."

Becky walked into eternal life with that perfect love for her Savior. *Love in Bloom!*

"ARISE AND SF

*"If my people, which are d
name, shall humble themselves   pray,
and seek my face, and turn from their
wicked ways; then will I hear from heaven,
and will forgive their sin, and will heal
their land*

—2 Chronicles 7:14

Can you picture Jesus standing at the right side
of God with hands outstretched toward his people,
you and me if we believe in him as our Lord and
Savior. He's talking to us! He's saying, "Come
alive, my people, arise, and shine for me." He
wants each of us to come to him as a little child,
humbly, and tell him about all the things we have
been doing and thinking that have been displeasing to him—those little insidious sins that we
haven't really wanted to call sin. We haven't even
wanted to think about them because we might
have to admit they are sins. We just tuck them
away back in the little drawers of our brain. They
go unconfessed and many of us go merrily on our
way, working even more and more for him. Consequently, we don't have time to seek his face. I

many Christians, if we took a poll,
en thirty minutes a day with the Lord in
e reading or prayer.

We continue to talk about how horrible the world situation is, we reiterate the terrible sins of the world, but we are doing nothing about it. We talk with this person and that one lamenting, "What is the answer?" Some even go so far as to say, "What can I do about world events?" We have heard the answer from many lips or, no doubt, have read it in the Bible. If we want our land healed, we must, as individuals as well as groups, draw near to God; then he will draw near to us. This is his answer.

Are you aware that God is speaking to us? He wants us to draw near to him, confess our sins, and turn from our wicked ways. Then, and *only* then, will he hear us, forgive us, and heal our world. My, isn't that a simple way to get out of this awful dilemma we have gotten ourselves into! Perhaps you are thinking, I'm not wicked. Maybe you think you aren't. Sometimes we as Christians fall into this snare. We categorize sin. We name certain things we believe to be sins. Since we are not guilty of these, we lull ourselves into a condition whereby we are not conscious of the fact that some of the things *we* are thinking and doing are displeasing to God.

Let's take a look at some of the things that God calls deadly sins. Read the sixth chapter of Proverbs. What does God say? A proud look. Oh, am I guilty of that? The other day I suddenly realized I had just committed that sin. Over the past six months I've lost twenty pounds and, naturally, I'm very happy about it. But at a moment when my guard was down, pride sneaked in. I looked at a woman who had too much fat around her middle and I began to think, "Oh, she's fat. I'm really proud of the way I look. This dress fits me very well now." That last word the Holy Spirit picked up and repeated for me—*now*, but you did look like she did. You're proud! Yes, I got the message. I had indulged in a quick proud look at myself. See how easy it is to sin.

Now take that sin of lying. Have you or do you go to the phone and say, "No, he isn't here at the moment. I'll have him call you." Now wait a minute. There he sits in his big easy chair reading the paper. When he heard the phone ring, he began motioning to you to tell them he isn't there. I hate to remind you both of this but you are *Christians* and you both are lying. Oh, yes, one more thing that enters into the picture. Johnny is sitting on the floor playing and his little ears are taking all this in. He thinks, "Mother and daddy are doing this. It must be all right." The next day you catch Johnny in a lie and you spank him for it. He's confused. He doesn't understand. He heard you and daddy lie last night. Often a person will ask another person to lie for him just as this daddy did. Watch this. Don't be taken in to lie for someone else. Your refusal in a sweet loving way can be a witness for Christ.

Another sin God lists here is imagining wicked things about others. This is one we really have to watch because it is so easy to permit our imaginations to devise untrue thoughts about others, especially about our own loved ones. When that very first thought tries to get in, you must reject it and quickly repeat a verse from the Bible you have learned. How about, "The Lord is my shepherd, I shall not want," for true and kind thoughts.

Another sin often overlooked is sowing discord among our sisters and brothers in Christ. Think on that one for a moment. It's so easy to do. You call Mary this morning because she is chairman of the decorations committee for your mother-daughter banquet. You have just heard from Jane that Helen, another member of the committee, isn't at all satisfied with the decorations you have suggested. As you talk you say, "I just felt, Mary, you needed to know this because it looks like you are headed for trouble, etc." This gets Mary all upset and then she's tempted and succumbs to sinning by saying some very critical things about Helen and on and on. This snowballs and the first thing you know Mary has resigned as chairman and all the committee members are angry with one another. There are numerous examples of this sin. Let's watch carefully that we do not have to plead guilty to this one.

Read, study, and think over the rest of those

deadly sins that God lists. Are you guilty of any of them? Perhaps God is convincing you of one of these this very moment. If so, confess it and get right with your heavenly Father. Perhaps you aren't having prayers answered. It may be because there is unconfessed sin in your life. I'm afraid Christians are taking the easy way out. The Christian type of life is not easy to live, but if we trust Christ to help us he becomes our way of living. Most of us think of sin as adultery, stealing, drinking, smoking, dancing. But God lists many others. Let's take another good look inside ourselves and confess so that God can use us in the healing process of our land.

When we have confessed our sins and desire to be a servant to God, we must be alive, filled with his Holy Spirit, so that those who do not know Christ as their Savior or friend will know just by looking at us and talking to us that we have something they would like to have. Are you alive? Are you bubbling? Are you so filled with God's Spirit you are spilling over into other people's lives?

Several years ago my husband and I were in Boston. He was taking a surgery course at Massachusetts General Hospital and since he had to leave early in the mornings, I usually had breakfast alone. While we were there Boston had one of its worst snowstorms. On this particular morning they were serving the breakfast buffet style since only a few waitresses had come in. When I got into the line at the buffet table I couldn't help but notice the elderly gentleman in front of me and hear the conversation going on between him and the hostess. Looking at his full plate and then at the hostess, he said, "I'm not counting my calories this morning. I'm counting my blessings." He was just radiating sparks of joy. Then he looked at me and I said, "Good morning, and you really look as if you believe it is." "Oh, I do believe it," he replied. As I took a place at a table across from him I couldn't help think, He has to be a Christian, he truly is full of the joy of the Lord. I longed to exchange a few words with him about the Lord but when he left the dining room before I did I believed the opportunity had passed for that.

Much to my surprise the Lord had other plans. When I walked to the elevator, there he stood. We got on together and I quickly said, "Are you going outside and brave the storm?" He said, "No, I'm happy no planes are flying out of here today, and I doubt if they will fly tomorrow either." He continued, "Before I left home I said to my wife, 'I just wish the Lord would shut me up in my room in Boston so I could rest before going on to New York.' That's just what he has done. Isn't the Lord wonderful?" By that time we had reached the lobby. We hadn't noticed the elevator had stopped and then begun its upward climb again. We were still talking about the Lord. After leaving each other I realized we hadn't asked each other's names but we didn't have to. I knew his name was Christian and he knew mine was the same.

Some Christians are spiritually contagious; others are not. Some are alive and shining forth in the corner where God has placed them. In 1959 while I was in the Holy Land this truth was brought to my attention. My friend Betty Scott, our Christian guide Jesse Shakra, and I were in the room in the home where Paul is supposed to have received the return of his eyesight. Jesse asked us if we would like to have prayer together. Betty and I thankfully agreed. In Jesse's prayer he asked that after Betty and I returned to the states God would make us "shine" for him. I hope in some measure I have fulfilled Jesse's petition for me.

Have you placed your light on a candlestick? All who come near my mother at eighty-six know she is burning brightly in the corner where God has put her. To be alive and to be shining means not only to serve but also to be obedient. Mother certainly proved this when several months ago she announced she would like to be baptized. Mother had been sprinkled when a child, and I wondered what had made her come to this decision. When I questioned her, she said she had heard a minister over the radio speak on the scriptural authority of immersion. As she meditated on this, the thought came to her that Jesus had set the example for us to follow in all things including water baptism. Suddenly she said she knew definitely that the Lord wanted her to be immersed. I was delighted and passed the word along to our pastor. When I related mother's desire to Becky, our daughter-in-law, she said she would love to be immersed at the same time grandma was.

Here again I wondered what was behind Becky's decision. She told me she had just read Pat Boone's book, *A New Song*. He tells about the many people who have been baptized in his swimming pool. She became very excited after reading this and began to think more and more about immersion in water as being symbolic of having our sins forgiven and accepting Jesus Christ as our Savior.

As I watched mother walk into the water of baptism, I knew I was witnessing a miracle, not only spiritual but physical. Mother never went near water of any kind during her lifetime. Here without any word of fear she was taking each step into the water on faith. I knew she was walking with her hand in the Lord's and trusting him all the way. A miracle, for mother is afflicted with arthritis and is almost blind with cataracts in both eyes! She came up out of the water with her face shining radiantly. I could see the wonderful peace on her face that only the Lord can give. Mother told me later that she was now ready to go to be with Jesus any time he called for her. Becky's face also shone with a holy radiance and she, too, stated the peace she felt from having obeyed the Lord. After the service, our minister told us that Mother was the oldest person he had ever had the privilege of baptizing and that she was also the oldest person ever to be baptized in our church.

All who witnessed this service felt the presence of the living God in our midst. Mother received a touching note from a dear friend of our family who was one of the witnesses. I received one from his wife. Mother and I would like to share these notes with you.

"Dear Grandma Melson: I have long been amazed at the degree to which you maintain contact with such a wide segment of the world outside 8914 Maravilla. Your letters and your 'shopping' and your interest shown in so many things, places, and people has been an inspiration to us all.

"But the best of all is to find that I have been recently within that special area of your concern. Your gift, your card, yes, your love, I will long remember and greatly appreciate. Thank you so much!

"One of the most meaningful incidents in which I ever took part was the occasion of your baptism that Sunday afternoon not so long ago. If ever such an event was actually graced by the presence of a loving, living God, it was that one. It was such a beautiful climax to a life of devotion. I am thankful to have been with you on that day.

"Thanks for all your thoughts and prayers. With love, Ted."

"Dear Betsy: One of the most thrilling events I have ever witnessed was the recent baptism of your Mother and Becky, your daughter-in-law. On the one hand was the beauty of the faith and wisdom of age, and on the other the innocence and joy of youth. Both had their trust in their Lord Jesus Christ and their belief that they should obey him in following him in the waters of baptism. Truly an inspiring moment! Lovingly, Betty."

Our family's reaction to this baptismal service was: what a precious sight to behold, the old and young being baptized together and this special blessing was ours! While witnessing this beautiful picture in our church, once again I realized there are no doors in heaven marked by any denominational title, but those of us who are his are all one in him. Praise the Lord!

To be alive and to serve our Lord in the most effective way we must be filled with the Holy Spirit. Some Christians truthfully do not know what that means. They have accepted Christ as their personal Savior and there they remain. They have stopped growing. They have not asked Jesus to fill them to overflowing with his Spirit. They have crawled into a box in their church with other busy Christians doing church work and they become very cuddly and cozy in that box together. They are so busy doing the Lord's work in the church that they become ineffective in their Christian life. They are not studying God's word; consequently not keeping his command in 2 Timothy 2:15, "Study to shew thyself approved unto God, a workman that needeth not to be ashamed, rightly dividing the word of truth." They are not spending time in prayer. Consequently they are not equipped to share Christ with others outside the church, and do not even try. We must be immersed in his Spirit. A minister illustrated this truth by using a sponge and a glass of water. When we receive salvation or accept Christ as our personal Savior, the sponge is dipped into the water. The Holy Spirit has come into our life, (into the foyer or front hall, shall we say), but when we ask God's Spirit to come into every area of our life, it is like immersing the sponge completely into the glass of water. When it is taken out it drips everywhere. Thus the Spirit-filled Christian is contagious. In a small atomic plant, a Geiger counter passed over a glass pond in which there were small turtles. Nothing happened when it passed over most of the turtles, but every time it came to one little turtle sparks would fly and noises would come from the machine. The little turtle was radioactive. Some Christians are like that. They are radioactive with the Holy Spirit and you feel the sparks from the Spirit hit you when you get near them. Peter and Paul were radioactive with the Holy Spirit. They said in Acts 4:20, "For we cannot but speak on the things which we have seen and heard." They just couldn't keep their mouths shut.

To be alive in Christ means you are using the sense of humor God has given you. Do you use yours? I read a little sign on a billboard that said, "A smile increases your face value." The Bible says, "A merry heart doeth good." My dear friend, Agnes Krick, calls something that makes one laugh "a tickle." Do you share with others funny little things; something that has made you laugh? What a good laugh will do for a person! Do you share your smiles and "tickles" freely?

An expression familiar to all of us is, "That church is dead." It is true that some of the people in our churches today are more dead than alive. In my opinion the greatest lie the devil is feeding people in our churches today is this: There are many roads on which we can travel to get to heaven. It doesn't matter which one you take. We are all working to go to the same place. This definitely is not truth. This is not what the Bible says. The Bible says through the words of Jesus: "I am the way, the truth, and the life: no man cometh unto the Father, but by me" (John 14:6). The Bible also says in Acts 4:12, that there is only one name on earth whereby we can be saved and that's the name Christ Jesus. To me these statements are pretty clear. The Bible also says we cannot work our way into heaven. In other words, we cannot get there by good works. Eternal life comes only by faith in Jesus Christ after confessing we are sinners and have sinned.

You will never meet a more exciting person than Jesus. If you want thrills in your life *now*, he is the One to know. A popular song says, "What the world needs now is love sweet love." No, what the world needs now is to come alive, to have faith in God through Jesus Christ, then love—real love—will come automatically. We won't have to work at it or whip it up.

My prayer and challenge to each of you wherever you may be is to be a positive influence on others for Christ. Come alive, rise, and shine!

As I complete his book I'm praising God for the privilege of being used in this way. I'm thanking him for fulfilling the first part of Job 19:23 which he gave me many years ago, "Oh that my words were now written!" The last part of the verse says, "Oh that they were printed in a book!" I know this *too* he will fulfill, "For he is faithful that promised" (Hebrews 10:23).

I had to go down into the valley of despair to find Christ, to have my eyes opened to the truth. In the valley I cried out to God for help. He heard my cry. He opened my eyes and gave me vision which included eternal life with him, forgiveness, peace, and oh, so much more. I've tried to share with you "this happening" in my life. If it hasn't happened to you, why not let it happen now!